Channels of His Spirit
A Study of The Acts of the Apostles

Horace R. Weaver and James C. Hares

Abingdon Press
Nashville and New York

CONTENTS

1. By My Spirit
(Acts 1)

In Acts you will learn how the first Christians used their Scriptures. You will see how they tied their Jewish Scriptures to their faith as Christians. You will discover what the apostles emphasized in their preaching. You will learn what portions of the Old Testament the apostles read most often to the congregations. You will come to know which prophets the apostles quoted most often. This study of Acts will show how the early church used the Old Testament. Finally, the Holy Spirit, who will be so important in this Bible study, is the guiding force throughout Acts.

Christians today need to know how the first Christians used their Scriptures. We must read the Old Testament as they did. So we turn to The Acts of the Apostles with expectancy. We are open to fresh challenges from God.

Let each reader of this book now turn to his Bible and read Acts 1.

WHO WROTE THE ACTS OF THE APOSTLES?
Acts 1:1-2

In the first book, O Theophilus, I have dealt with all that Jesus began to do and teach, until the day when he was taken up, after he had given commandment through the Holy Spirit to the apostles whom he had chosen.

Who is *I* in Acts 1:1? The Scriptures do not say. But several early church leaders (Irenaeus, Tertullian, and Clement) stated that Luke the physician was the writer. They identified the writer of Acts with Paul's friend, the beloved physician named in Colossians 4:14. (See also 2 Timothy 4:11 and Philemon 24.)

Bible students have long noted that similar concerns appear both in Luke's Gospel and in Acts. Both books, for example, show a compassion for the poor. Luke seems to be the writer of both books. Together they are a two-volume work: (1) The Gospel According to Luke and (2) The Acts of the Apostles.

The apostles was first church

Think what it means to us that Luke was probably the writer. Think of Luke, a physician who lived over ten years as Paul's friend. He spent twenty years working with leaders of the early church. He knew Peter, James, Lydia, Priscilla, and Timothy. He saw Paul on trial before Agrippa II and Felix. Luke took part in the Christian fellowships at Corinth, Athens, Antioch, Caesarea, Troas, Ephesus, Philippi, and Rome. He knew their weaknesses and strengths. He received the Lord's Supper with them. He prayed with them. And he witnessed with them to their faith under trying circumstances. He knew what they said and believed about Jesus. He knew how they interpreted their Scriptures. He saw the Holy Spirit at work in each of these churches. He knew what it meant to them to be channels of the Holy Spirit. He was able to get firsthand accounts of how the church began. He knew directly what the early church was like.

To whom did Luke write? Why did he write? In Acts 1:1 he addresses Theophilus. Perhaps Luke did not address one specific person. The Greek word *Theophilus* means "lover of God." Luke could have been writing to everyone who loves God, including us. Or Theophilus may have bee⸺⸺⸺⸺⸺d affectionate name for some Roman official. C⸺⸺⸺⸺s Flavius Clemens, a cousin to Emperor Domitian an⸺⸺⸺ole heir to the Roman Empire. Flavius' wife Domitilla was known to be a Christian. Was Luke reporting to his Roman friend and benefactor Flavius Clemens about the work in which his wife was deeply involved? Though we do not know for sure, either view (or possibly both) may be true.

Luke wrote his Gospel to give Theophilus an accurate account of the life, teachings, deeds, death, and resurrection of Jesus. (See Luke 1:1-4.) Luke wrote Acts to tell Theophilus how faith in the risen Christ under the leadership of the Holy Spirit moved beyond Jerusalem to Rome. Like ripples made by a stone dropped on the surface of a quiet pond, the faith moved in widening circles. The faith spread from Jerusalem to Samaria, to Antioch, to Asia Minor, to Africa, to Rome, and throughout the world.

THE KINGDOM OF GOD
Acts 1:3-8

So when they had come together, they asked him, "Lord, will you at this time restore the kingdom to Israel?" He said to them, "It is not for you to know times or seasons which the Father has fixed by his own authority. But you shall receive power when

The globe and the cross held by Christ represent his Lordship over the whole earth.

The Ascension, by Albrecht Durer
The Cleveland Museum of Art, Gift of Hanna Fund

the Holy Spirit has come upon you; and you shall be my witnesses in Jerusalem and in all Judea and Samaria and to the end of the earth." (Acts 1:6-8)

In these verses Luke described a meeting of apostles and disciples with the risen Lord. Jesus spoke of the Kingdom during his life. Now after his resurrection he spoke again of the Kingdom. He had in mind the *kingdom of God,* but the disciples asked about the restoration of the *kingdom to Israel.* The disciples asked, "Will you at this time restore the kingdom to Israel?" This question must have hurt Jesus. The disciples had heard his words, but they had missed his *meaning.* They still thought first of personal position and power. They did not understand what Jesus had taught and was still teaching about the Kingdom. Jesus had taught that the Kingdom comes not by force and coercion but by the persuasive power of God's Spirit. It comes like leaven in dough, spreading through the whole loaf and lifting it slowly but surely. The disciples thought in terms of thrones, cabinet seats, and political maneuvers. They thought still of national glory. Yet Jesus taught that the kingdom of God has to do with what and how men think. Read Matthew 13:24-33, 44-52 for a sample of his ideas about the Kingdom.

Jesus answered their question indirectly. He pointed out that only God could really answer their question. (See Acts 1:6-7.) Jesus then answered their request for power by referring to power of a different kind. Like Zechariah, he spoke of the power of the Holy Spirit. "Not by might, nor by power, but by my Spirit says the LORD of hosts." (Zechariah 4:6) Jesus said, "You shall receive power when the Holy Spirit has come upon you." (Acts 1:8) *The Kingdom would come as men received God's Holy Spirit, witnessed to his purposes, and became instruments of his peace.*

In his first sermon in Nazareth, Jesus turned to Isaiah 61:1-2*a* and read to the members of his synagogue:

"The Spirit of the Lord is upon me,
because he has anointed me to preach good news to the poor.
He has sent me to proclaim release to the captives
and recovering of sight to the blind,
to set at liberty those who are oppressed. . . ."

(See Luke 4:16-19.) We must not overlook the meaning of the clause *the Spirit of the Lord is upon me.*

Jesus knew that his disciples did not have this Spirit within them. Before Pentecost they were not yet Christian in purpose, attitude, or commitment. But the Spirit would come. (We might face our own lives at this point. Do we share Jesus' vision of the kingdom of God? Do we share his vision of that special power that comes only from the Spirit? Do we expect the Kingdom on God's terms?)

One of the characteristics we admire in John and Charles Wesley is a Christlike concern for the poor, the imprisoned, and the broken-hearted. We admire the Wesleys because we see the Holy Spirit in their lives. Remember that John Wesley waited many years before the Holy Spirit came upon his life. Jesus asked his disciples to wait to receive the Spirit.

A person in whom the Holy Spirit dwells will always care about the afflicted, the imprisoned, and the poor. He will fulfill Isaiah 61:1-4. In his life the kingdom of God will come once more. (For a list of other fruits of the Spirit, see Galatians 5:22-23.)

Today the risen Christ seeks new channels, new minds, new persons through whom the purposes of God can work. The church receives power when it says *Yes* to our Lord's call to discipleship. A dead church is simply a group of people who refuse the leadership of the Spirit. To refuse his Spirit means to refuse his attitudes toward our fellow men and God.

Though many persons in Jesus' day were converted, they had not yet received his Spirit. Their spirits were still poverty-stricken. Instead of thinking about the purposes of God, they still thought of political opportunism, military might, and positions of authority. Yet when the Spirit comes we are transformed by the renewal of our minds, and we prove the will of God by living it. (See Romans 12:2.) We need God's scheme of spiritual values.

Yes, the risen Christ calls to each of us to accept him. Let us accept his concerns as our concerns and his ways as our ways. Only as we say *Yes* to his Spirit are we truly Christians.

THE MEANING OF THE ASCENSION FOR US
Acts 1:9-11

> And when he had said this, as they were looking on, he was lifted up, and a cloud took him out of their sight. And while they were gazing into heaven as he went, behold, two men stood by them in white robes, and said, "Men of Galilee, why do you stand looking into heaven? This Jesus, who was taken up from you into heaven, will come in the same way as you saw him go into heaven."

When people in our day read this passage, they find it hard to understand what happened. The disciples probably believed in a flat earth. The sky that covered the flat earth spread out like a huge tent or dome. The stars and the planets moved across the heavens. Christ could go up beyond the dome to God's throne. We know scientifically that this was a mistaken view. The earth is more like a sphere than like a plane. The heavens are endless, holding galaxy after galaxy and uncounted planetary systems. We ask, Is there a physical place with a physical throne where Jesus sits somewhere in the heavens above the sky? How can we think about the ascension of Jesus when we no longer believe in a flat earth or in a throne of God above the sky?

The Scriptures refer to a *cloud* and to *heaven*. (See Acts 1:9-10.) We need to ask if other Scriptures might shed light on these words. The answer is *Yes*. We must keep in mind that the early Christians thought in biblical terms. They sometimes used symbols to express what they could not explain in words. The word *cloud* may be such a symbol. Time and again in the Bible the "cloud" is a signal of God's presence and glory. Let us recall several instances.

Ezekiel during a sandstorm knew the presence of God. "As I looked, behold, a stormy wind came out of the north, and a great *cloud,* with brightness round about it, and *fire* flashing forth continually." (Ezekiel 1:4, italics added)

The Hebrew words for *cloud* and *fire* are the same words Moses used to express his awareness of the presence of God. The fire that Moses saw in the burning bush represented the presence of God. (See Exodus 3:2-6.)

Similarly, a cloud and fire were symbols for God's presence at the tent of meeting during the wilderness wanderings. "When Moses entered the tent, the pillar of cloud would descend and stand at the door of the tent, and the Lord would speak with Moses." (Exodus 33:9) The cloud that hovered over the tent of meeting indicated God's presence with Moses.

So God was present when "a cloud took him [Jesus] out of their sight." (Acts 1:9)

The disciples knew as we do that the resurrected Lord is continually in the presence of God. They knew that wherever God is, Jesus is there also. But the disciples, all Jews, had learned in their sabbath schools that God resides in heaven. Heaven is his throne, and the earth is his footstool. (See Isaiah 66:1-2.)

So we may reason as follows. We know God is Spirit. We know the risen Lord is Spirit. We may reason that God and Christ do not require a physical place to live. Being Spirit, they are in the kingdom of heaven. So we may regard the Ascension as a moment when the resurrected Jesus withdrew from earthly limitations and became free to be present everywhere at the same time. Time and space no longer set limits to his activity.

One of our astronauts partook of the Lord's Supper while he was on the moon. At the same time his family communed in their church in a small town in the United States. Time and space are not barriers to the risen Christ.

God promised Moses, "My presence will go with you." (Exodus 33:14) Moses responded, "Is it not in thy going with us . . . that we are distinct, I and thy people, from all other people that are upon the face of the earth?" (Exodus 33:16) So Christians find this experience of the risen Lord unique to faith. "Lo, I am with you always" (Matthew 28:20) is a great promise and assurance to faith.

Many Christians hold another view of the Ascension. Thousands of Christians hold to the literal ascension of Jesus from earth to a heaven above the sky. They accept devoutly and literally the idea that Jesus is seated physically at the right hand of God. As he went up, so he will come down on the clouds at the Second Coming.

How do we deal with the wide variety of beliefs about the Ascension?

At this point Christians should recall John Wesley's spirit of openness. For example, in one of his letters he stated that he disagreed heartily with the beliefs of Quakers. They did not observe the Lord's Supper or hold to the Apostles' Creed. Yet, said Wesley, they love God and their neighbors. He could not withold the name *Christian* from them.

So we too, no matter which view of the Acension we hold, need to recognize that we are free to differ from others in the way we interpret our Bible. Yet we all strive to love God and our neighbors as ourselves. We offer our hands in fellowship to one another as we receive and follow the risen Christ. All of us agree that Jesus is where God is. We agree that his authority is above all others. He is "seated at the right hand of God." He is worthy of our worship, love, and attentive hearing. The risen Lord is King and Savior.

We should observe further that persons who hold to either of these views of the Ascension claim that God made our world with a grand design. The universe is going somewhere. It is moving in accord with the divine plan. God's purpose can be defeated for a moment, but not finally. God and his will shall prevail. Purposes that conflict with those held by the risen Lord defeat themselves. They do not defeat God. The kingdom of this world shall become the kingdom of our Christ.

Read carefully and thoughtfully the rest of Acts 1. Verses 13-26 tell of the choosing of a twelfth apostle to replace Judas Iscariot. In verses 21-22, note the basic requirement for being chosen an apostle. Then ask yourself: Am I responding to his call to permit his Holy Spirit to rest on my motives and life? Am I a witness to the Resurrection?

2. Power to the People of God
(Acts 2:1 through 2:41)

Just before his Ascension (when he was taken from the sight of his disciples), Jesus made a request. He asked the disciples to stay together until they received the Holy Spirit. "You shall receive power when the Holy Spirit has come upon you; and you shall be my witnesses. . . ." (Acts 1:8)

The disciples stayed together for fifty days between Passover and Pentecost. What did they do for these seven weeks? They were probably together all the time in fellowship and in singing. They also praised God for their experience of the presence of Jesus after the Resurrection. They prayed in the temple and discussed the meaning of their Scripture (our Old Testament). They tried to relate the Old Testament to Jesus. They read again the writings of their prophets and realized that they were seeing ancient hopes and prophecies fulfilled in their own day. They knew that a fresh bond between God and man, *a new covenant,* was being born.

Now read all of Acts 2 from your Bible.

A NEW CREATIVE ACT OF GOD
Acts 2:1-3

When the day of Pentecost had come, they were all together in one place. And suddenly a sound came from heaven like the rush of a mighty wind, and it filled all the house where they were sitting. And there appeared to them tongues as of fire, distributed and resting on each one of them.

Pentecost, a harvest festival, ended a season of seven weeks that began with Passover. During this season and on these holy days, the Jews remembered two events. The first was God's redemption of Israel from Egypt. The second was God's gift of the law to Israel at Mount Sinai.

As we noted earlier, the disciples during these seven weeks read their Scriptures with fresh understanding. They thought about the death and resurrection of Jesus in the light of prophecy.

One of their favorite prophets was Isaiah of Babylon, whose writings are found in Isaiah 40 through 55. Isaiah of Babylon prophesied to the exiles about 540 B.C.

"I am the Lord, your Holy One,
    the Creator of Israel, your King."
Thus says the Lord,
    who makes a way in the sea,
    a path in the mighty waters,
who brings forth chariot and horse,
    army and warrior;
they lie down, they cannot rise,
    they are extinguished, quenched like a wick:
"Remember not the former things,
    nor consider the things of old.
Behold, I am doing a new thing;
    now it springs forth, do you not perceive it?
I will make a way in the wilderness
    and rivers in the desert." (Isaiah 43:15-19)

Think how these words from Isaiah must have excited the disciples.

Through the Exodus from Egypt, God redeemed Israel. Isaiah recalls this event in verses 15-17. And Isaiah promises a new redemption, a new exodus, in verses 18-19. The disciples believed that God was fulfilling Isaiah's promise in their day. God was leading a new exodus, a new redemption. This new redemption was not just an exodus from an enemy land. It was an exodus from sin. The prophet said, "Sing to the LORD a new song." (Isaiah 42:10) No wonder the early church wrote new songs. And so do we, for the same reason. God is moving redemptively among us even as he moved among our fathers in the faith.

During the festival of Pentecost, the early Christians thought about the covenant and the giving of the law. They also read in Jeremiah about a new covenant. They must have seen that God was fulfilling the promise in Jeremiah 31:31-34.

Jeremiah lived when the Book of Deuteronomy was found in the temple. (See 2 Kings 22 through 23.) Soon King Josiah made Deu-

Christ on the Cross, by Albrecht Durer
Courtesy of The Art Institute of Chicago

This picture shows Mary, the mother of Jesus, and John, the beloved disciple, as well as Christ.

teronomy the religious law of the land (621 B.C.). As the years passed, Jeremiah saw the futility of what Josiah had tried to do. The king had tried to legislate virtue and goodness. Obeying external rules (like the Ten Commandments) cannot make men new. So Jeremiah dreamed of a better day and a better way. He wrote this prophetic promise:

> "Behold, the days are coming, says the Lord, when I will make a new covenant with the house of Israel and the house of Judah, not like the covenant which I made with their fathers when I took them by the hand to bring them out of the land of Egypt. . . . But this is the covenant which I will make with the house of Israel after those days, says the Lord: I will put my law within them, and I will write it upon their hearts; and I will be their God, and they shall be my people." (Jeremiah 31:31-33)

God through Jeremiah promises a new covenant. God no longer will write his laws on tablets of stone. Instead he will write them in the motives and thoughts (hearts) of men. A new world will come. A new creation, a new era, new creatures will appear.

God made the same promise through Ezekiel, a prophet who lived at the same time as Jeremiah. "A new heart I will give you, and a new spirit I will put within you." (Ezekiel 36:26)

The disciples also remembered how the Lord Jesus as he left them had said, "I send the promise of my Father upon you; but stay in the city, until you are clothed with power from on high."

(Luke 24:49) They believed that this new power, the Holy Spirit, would come soon.

Then, as they had hoped, the miracle happened. God gave them more than an intellectual understanding of prophecy. He gave them an actual experience of the Holy Spirit, who came just as Jesus had promised.

How does one describe in words what God did at Pentecost? God created a new kind of man, the Spirit-filled follower of the risen Christ. Just as he had once created the heavens and the earth, so at Pentecost God created a new humanity. By his creative power, a new era began.

Naturally the early Christians thought, as you and I would, of the creation story in Genesis. In Genesis 1:2 we read that the Spirit of God was moving over the face of the deep. One Hebrew word, *ruach,* may be translated as either *spirit* or *breath* or *wind.* One recent translation of Genesis 1:2 reads: "The *wind* of God moved over the face of the deep." The wind and the breath of God are symbols for the person of God himself. God moved over the depths to create the heavens and the earth. In this same creative spirit (wind, breath) God moves over the depths of the lives of persons and creates new personalities. Peter, James, and John knew this. They felt the changes within that the Spirit made as he hovered over their lives. Such was the experience at Pentecost, fifty days after the resurrection of Jesus.

Later, John described in his Gospel this same "breath of God," "wind of God," Spirit of God.

When he had said this, he showed them his hands and his side. Then the disciples were glad when they saw the Lord. Jesus said to them again, "Peace be with you. As the Father has sent me, even so I send you." And when he had said this, he breathed on them and said to them, "Receive the Holy Spirit." (John 20:20-22)

THE ETERNAL FIRE

"And there appeared to them tongues as of fire, distributed and resting on each one of them." (Acts 2:3) Again we turn to other passages of Scripture to help us understand this passage. The phrase *tongues as of fire* reminds us of Moses' experience. He saw a bush burning with fire, but the bush was not consumed. That symbol is still used by thousands of synagogues in our day.

Words are not enough to explain the unexplainable. So we use metaphors such as "fire" or "flame" to express what we feel. The disciples at Pentecost were certain that God was among them. We need not assume that a flame (tongue of fire) literally came to rest over the head of each person. But we know that the disciples felt their hearts strangely warmed. They became aware of God and his love. Now various Scripture passages fitted together and made sense to them. Now the author of the Word spoke to their hearts in revealing ways.

John Wesley felt this same "flame of fire" as his heart was strangely warmed at Aldersgate. Perhaps you have felt this. Or perhaps you have seen others whose faces were flushed with a warm glow that showed their awareness of God's presence.

Pentecost, the birthday of the church, was an experience of God's fire welding a group of individuals together. They became the body of Christ.

THEY BEGAN TO SPEAK IN OTHER TONGUES
Acts 2:4-13

And they were all filled with the Holy Spirit and began to speak in other tongues, as the Spirit gave them utterance.

Now there were dwelling in Jerusalem Jews, devout men from every nation under heaven. And at this sound the multitude came together, and they were bewildered, because each one heard them speaking in his own language. (Acts 2:4-6)

We hear a lot these days about speaking in unknown tongues. What is this experience? Is this what happened at Pentecost? A study of 1 Corinthians 14 will help us understand Paul's view of "tongues." It also will help us understand what happened at Pentecost when the disciples "began to speak in other tongues."

Let us study carefully the distinctions that Paul makes between prophesying and speaking in tongues. (Read 1 Corinthians 14.)

(1) "For one who speaks in a tongue speaks not to men but to God; for no one understands him. . . . On the other hand, he who prophesies speaks to men for their upbuilding and encouragement and consolation." (1 Corinthians 14:2-3)

(2) "He who speaks in a tongue edifies himself, but he who prophesies edifies the church." (1 Corinthians 14:4)

(3) "If you in a tongue utter speech that is not intelligible, how will anyone know what is said? For you will be speaking into the air. There are doubtless many different languages in the world, and none is without meaning; but if I do not know the meaning of the language, I shall be a foreigner to the speaker and the speaker a foreigner to me." (1 Corinthians 14:9-11)

(4) "If . . . the whole church assembles and all speak in tongues and outsiders or unbelievers enter, will they not say that you are mad? But if all prophesy, and an unbeliever or outsider enters, he is convicted by all, he is called to account by all, . . . he will worship God and declare that God is really among you." (1 Corinthians 14:23-25)

Luke in Acts 2:4-11 makes it clear that Pentecost for Christians is a matter of prophesying, not speaking in unknown tongues. Luke points to Peter's sermon at Pentecost. (See Acts 2:14-21.) Peter sees in the events of Pentecost the fulfillment of Joel's prophecy, "your sons and your daughters shall prophesy." (Joel 2:28) This "prophesying" is what was taking place among the Christians.

Luke's description of what went on at Pentecost (Acts 2) does not harmonize with Paul's descriptions of "speaking in tongues." When they "began to speak in other tongues," each listener "heard them speaking in his own language." (Acts 2:4, 6) "Speaking in tongues" would not have been intelligible. So this was a time of prophesying. The Parthians, Medes, Elamites, and people from Cappadocia, Pontus, Asia, and Egypt (all Jews) said, "We hear them [the disciples] telling in our own tongues the mighty works of God." (Acts 2:11) This was *prophesying,* not speaking in tongues.

This passage may have another meaning too. It suggests that the confusion of tongues described in Genesis 11:1-9 is canceled at Pentecost. Genesis 11:1-9 tells us about ambitious men who built a temple (a "tower") in Shinar or Babylonia. They decided to build it higher than any other temple in the country. Its tower would be so high it would reach into the sky. They said, "Come, let us build ourselves a city, and a tower with its top in the heavens, and let us make a name for ourselves." (Genesis 11:4) Their motive was to honor themselves, not God.

Such pride in self-achievement divides men from one another. Pride keeps men from understanding one another. Genesis 11:7 says God confused their language and scattered them abroad. They could not understand one another.

At Pentecost the reverse happened. Men began to speak and to hear with understanding. Men from every nation under heaven were there. Each spoke in his own native language. But all (thousands) *understood what was being said.* The church of Jesus Christ was built out of love for God, not out of pride of self. When love, joy, gratitude, and loyalty to God build his church, then alienation and separation disappear.

Further, not just the old men and young men, but also the daughters prophesied. This was positive proof of a new day. Little

18

wonder that Paul told the Corinthians they should "earnestly desire to prophesy." (1 Corinthians 14:39) Prophecy brings outsiders into a living relationship with the risen Lord. (See 1 Corinthians 14:23-25.)

Some bystanders thought the people of the new covenant were drunk. Drunk? Yes, but not with new wine. They were men intoxicated with God's Spirit. They had experienced the new birth. They had become new creatures—Spirit-filled men and women. A new vision, a new hope, a new covenant, a new redemption were theirs. A new light had shone out of darkness. They were excited, illumined, proclaiming people. They now spoke to one another with understanding. They turned to their fellow countrymen and proclaimed the good news—now. They knew themselves to be sons of the new covenant. They were twice-born men. God had breathed new life into them. They were more than flesh and blood. They were Spirit-filled sons of the covenant.

THE PROCLAMATION OF THE GOSPEL
Acts 2:14-41

> "Men of Israel, hear these words: Jesus of Nazareth, a man attested to you by God with mighty works and wonders and signs which God did through him in your midst, as you yourselves know—this Jesus, delivered up according to the definite plan and foreknowledge of God, you crucified and killed by the hands of lawless men. But God raised him up, having loosed the pangs of death, because it was not possible for him to be held by it.
>
> ". . . This Jesus God raised up, and of that we all are witnesses. Being therefore exalted at the right hand of God, and having received from the Father the promise of the Holy Spirit, he has poured out this which you see and hear. . . . Let all the house of Israel therefore know assuredly that God has made him both Lord and Christ, this Jesus whom you crucified." (Acts 2:22-24, 32-33, 36)

Try to imagine the excitement of Peter and his fellow Christians as they explained what was taking place in their lives that morning. Peter proclaims four basic ideas (often called the *kerygma* of the church). (1) Jesus fulfills Old Testament prophecy. (2) The deeds, the life style, and the teachings of Jesus are signs of who he is. (3) God has raised Jesus from the dead. Therefore he is the Messiah. (4) Jesus is also Lord.

Let us briefly observe these four proclamations one a'

(1) Peter declared that Jesus ushered in a new age—a ¦ kind. A few years later Paul said that Jesus was the second

a new creature, a new man. (See 1 Corinthians 15:45-50.) Peter proclaimed that the message of the prophet Joel was being fulfilled in Jesus. (Joel 2:28-32) The "pouring out" of his Spirit upon women as well as men, upon young men as well as old, fulfills the dream: "I will pour out my Spirit; and they shall prophesy." (Acts 2:18)

(2) The deeds, the life style, and the teachings of Jesus tell us he is Messiah. "Jesus of Nazareth [is] a man attested to you by God with mighty works and wonders and signs which God did through him in your midst." (Acts 2:22) Luke and Matthew both present Jesus as the greatest man who ever lived. God worked in and through him far more than he did through Moses. Truly a man greater than Moses was in their midst. (See Deuteronomy 18:15.)

(3) "This Jesus God raised up, and of that we all are witnesses." (Acts 2:32) The Resurrection is God's proof that Jesus is the "Anointed One," that is, the Messiah. God completed his plan for Jesus by lifting him from the grave. Therefore we know Jesus as our Lord, Christ, and Savior.

(4) He is "exalted at the right hand of God." (Acts 2:33) He has more authority than King David, who (as Peter interpreted Psalms 16:8-11 and 110:1) called Jesus "Lord." (See Acts 2:25-28.) Furthermore, "God has made him both Lord and Christ, this Jesus whom you crucified." (Acts 2:36)

Peter's proclamation rested on the following foundations: (1) his new interpretation of Hebrew *Scriptures,* (2) his sense of fulfillment of the hopes of Jewish *tradition* for a coming Messiah, (3) his ecstatic *experience* of the presence of the risen Lord, and (4) the sheer *reasonableness* of God's most recent "mighty act."

Those non-Christians who had witnessed the change in the lives of Peter and the others could not contain themselves. They asked, "What shall we do?"

Peter responded, "Repent, and be baptized every one of you in the name of Jesus Christ for the forgiveness of your sins." (Acts 2:38)

The Jewish festival of harvest (a part of Pentecost) dramatized the act of "bringing in the sheaves" of harvest to God. So now the Christian Pentecost included celebrating harvest—a harvest of three thousand souls. Without such a harvest, the sense of personal awareness of God's Holy Spirit would have been empty indeed. A new life was ahead, a life of sharing, concern, compassion, mission. Life had just begun!

Study Here

3. Sons of the Covenant
(*Acts 2:42 through 6:7*)

We have studied about the birth of the church at Pentecost. We think of this event as the first feast of the new covenant. The feast of the old covenant (Jewish Pentecost) celebrated the giving of the law. So the feast of the new covenant (Christian Pentecost) celebrated the giving of the Holy Spirit.

The disciples continued to meet together after Pentecost. Who were their leaders? What kinds of sermons did the leaders preach? How was the church organized?

Read Acts 2:42 through 6:7 before you read the following paragraphs.

THE EARLY CHRISTIAN FELLOWSHIP
Acts 2:42-47

And they devoted themselves to the apostles' teaching and fellowship, to the breaking of bread and the prayers. . . . And day by day, attending the temple together and breaking bread in their homes, they partook of food with glad and generous hearts. . . . (Acts 2:42, 46)

When we think about what the early Christians did, we must remember that the Holy Spirit dwelt in them. The Holy Spirit within them dominated their preaching, guided all their activities, and shaped their concerns.

Let us notice what the Christians did in these first few weeks. (1) They listened to the apostles teach. The apostles taught both in the temple and in homes. (2) They devoted themselves to fellowship. The word *fellowship* means sharing and participation. By sharing they showed forth the Spirit that possessed them. Also, each one joined in thinking through their common faith. (3) And "fear came upon every soul." (Acts 2:43) The Hebrew word for *fear* is an ab-

21

CHANNELS OF HIS SPIRIT

breviation for the phrase *fear of the Lord*. This phrase means "religion." The psalmist wrote, "The fear of the Lord [religion or faith] is the beginning of wisdom." (Psalms 111:10)

The new converts learned more each day about the risen Christ. They began to find new meanings in their old Scriptures.

The first Christians were sensitive to other Christians in need. When they broke bread together, they also broke open their pocketbooks. They "had all things in common; and they sold their possessions and goods and distributed them to all, as any had need." (Acts 2:44-45)

Read Acts 4:32 through 5:11 for another statement by Luke about communal living.

Luke tells the story of Joseph Barnabas and Ananias. These two men sold their possessions, but each responded differently to the communal needs. Barnabas gave all that he had. He dramatized his unity with the brethren by sharing his property. But apparently Ananias was not sure how long the new movement would last. So he kept some money back to be on the safe side. Sapphira, his wife, then made his decision her own.

We need not conclude from Acts 4:32 through 5:11 that the Christians were building a new economic order. God does not expect all Christians today to pool their earnings and draw from a common treasury to pay their daily expenses. The first Christians waited for the End of the Age to come at any moment. Goods and money were not important to them. But the physical needs of other Christians were important.

THE FAITH WHICH IS THROUGH JESUS CHRIST
Acts 3

Read Acts 3. Here we see the faith of the early church in action. Peter and John (son of Zebedee) had been at either the Mount of Olives or Bethany. They walked toward the Gate Beautiful. They planned to enter the temple for their evening prayers at 3:00 P.M. They met a lame man who was begging. God healed the beggar when Peter took him by the hand and said, "In the name of Jesus Christ of Nazareth, walk." The healing boldly declared Peter's faith that Jesus was the Messiah. This healing fulfilled one of the promises in Isaiah 35:5-6.

> **Then the eyes of the blind shall be opened,**
> **and the ears of the deaf unstopped;**
> **then shall the lame man leap like a hart,**
> **and the tongue of the dumb sing for joy.**

What a sight the healed man was to the worshipers as they gathered for prayer that afternoon! "And leaping up he stood and walked and entered the temple with them, walking and *leaping* and *praising* God." (Acts 3:8, italics added) The man who had been healed clung to Peter and John. He also danced and leaped and shouted *hallelujah* (praise God). Soon a crowd gathered around them. Peter at once declared that this healing was the work of the Messiah.

HEALING IN THE NAME OF THE MESSIAH
Acts 3:12-26

> **"But you denied the Holy and Righteous One . . . And his name, by faith in his name, has made this man strong whom you see and know. . . .**
>
> **"And now, brethren, I know that you acted in ignorance, as did also your rulers. But what God foretold by the mouth of all the prophets, that his Christ [Messiah] should suffer, he thus fulfilled. Repent therefore. . . . Moses said, 'The Lord God will raise up for you a prophet from your brethren as he raised me up. . . .' . . . You are the sons of the prophets and of the covenant which God gave to your fathers. . . ."** (Acts 3:14, 16, 17-19, 22, 25)

The Old Testament refers to God as the "Holy One." Peter identified Jesus with God by calling him the *Holy One.*

The righteous one is also a phrase from the Old Testament. The prophet Isaiah of Babylon used the phrase *the righteous one.* (Read Isaiah 53.) Isaiah foresaw a righteous servant whose life of suffering for others would lead many men into righteousness. (See Isaiah 53:11.) Peter said that Jesus is the "righteous one" whom Isaiah expected. Surely, Jesus himself made this identification when he told his disciples that the Son of Man must *suffer* and *die.* (See Mark 8:27-33.)

By the time of Peter, Jewish traditions included many titles for the expected Messiah. Among them are these three phrases—*the Holy One, the Righteous One, the Author of life.* We see Peter using each of these in Acts 3:14-15. Peter proclaimed that Jesus was the Messiah who suffered and died for man's redemption. Jesus suffered because this was God's way of reclaiming and redeeming his people, who had broken their covenant. Through his suffering, men were being healed, fulfilling Isaiah 52:13 through 53:12. So through the "name" of Jesus (the continuing presence and power of the Messiah), the lame man could leap for joy.

Scripture and tradition uphold Peter's claim that Jesus was the Messiah. The experiences of men such as John, Peter, Stephen, and Paul also support this claim. This claim appeals to our reason too.

We fail to find any titles other than Lord, Christ, Messiah, the Righteous One, the Holy One of Israel that are more appropriate to Jesus' life, death, and resurrection. In Jesus, a prophet greater than Moses has come. (See Deuteronomy 18:15 and Acts 3:22.)

Peter pointed out (Acts 3:25) that Jesus is the fulfillment of the covenant God made with Abraham. Jesus is the One through whom God will bless all the families of the earth. (See Genesis 12:3b and Acts 3:25-26.) The followers of Jesus now inherit the promises and blessings of the covenant.

Recall that Peter spoke to men who came to the temple to seek the Lord. His message was as prophetic as the message of Isaiah of Babylon, who cried out:

"Hearken to me, you who pursue deliverance,
    you who seek the Lord;
look to the rock from which you were hewn,
    and to the quarry from which you were digged.
Look to Abraham your father
    and to Sarah who bore you. . . ." (Isaiah 51:1-2a)

In brief, Peter was saying: Remember you are sons of the covenant. Don't forget your spiritual heritage and spiritual ancestors. Don't forget your roots. He asked each person to renew his own covenant with God. Peter knew well the ancient claim in Deuteronomy 5:2-3. That passage tells each Jew to experience personally the redemption God gave his fathers.

"The Lord our God made a covenant with us in Horeb [Sinai]. Not with our fathers did the Lord make this covenant, but with us, who are all of us here alive this day." (Deuteronomy 5:2-3)

Note the emphasis on personal experience—*with us, who are all of us here alive this day*. The Jews were sons of the covenant. But we Christians are sons of the new covenant, established by Christ and possessed by faith. (Acts 3:16)

HOW THE EARLY CHRISTIANS DEALT WITH CONFLICT
Acts 4

Then Peter, filled with the Holy Spirit, said to them, "Rulers of the people and elders, if we are being examined today concerning a good deed done to a cripple, by what means this man has been healed, be it known to you all, and to all the people

Peter and John at the Beautiful Gate of the Temple
By Rembrandt van Ryn
Courtesy of The Art Institute of Chicago

25

of Israel, that by the name of Jesus Christ of Nazareth, whom
you crucified, whom God raised from the dead, by him this man
is standing before you well. This is the stone which was rejected
by you builders, but which has become the head of the corner.
And there is salvation in no one else, for there is no other name
under heaven given among men by which we must be saved."
(Acts 4:8-12)

In order to understand the arrest of Peter and John, their courage,
and their witness, read Acts 4.

Peter's preaching annoyed the priests (Caiaphas and Annas), the
temple guard, and the Sadducees. The annoyance was caused by a
theological conflict. The Sadducees did not believe in resurrection
at all. So they hotly denied Peter's tale of Jesus' resurrection. They
also denied Peter's claim that the Resurrection confirmed God's
choice of Jesus as Messiah.

Peter witnessed to the Sanhedrin, saying that the lame man at the
Gate Beautiful had found healing (salvation) in the name of Christ.
Finding no way to condemn them, the officials released Peter and
John. But they told Peter and John to keep silent about Jesus.

The prayer in Acts 4:24-30 is the prayer offered by the church
after Peter and John were released. It is the first recorded prayer of
the early church face to face with conflict. Study the prayer carefully. What were the Christians asking of God?

"And now, Lord, look upon their threats, and grant to thy servants
to speak thy word with all boldness, while thou stretchest out
thy hand to heal, and signs and wonders are performed through
the name of thy holy servant, Jesus." (Acts 4:29-30)

They asked for boldness *to speak*. They also asked for healing for
their enemies. The word *salvation* comes from a root word that means
"healing." They prayed that their enemies might be healed, saved
by the Lord Jesus Christ. This is great praying. In verse 31 we discover that, as they prayed, God gave them a powerful sign of his
presence.

Little wonder that the next verse says, "Now the company of those
who believed were of one heart and soul." (Acts 4:32) The believers
were at one with one another and with God because they had accepted atonement and because they had prayed for their enemies,
the Sanhedrin.

"SING THEM OVER AGAIN TO ME, WONDERFUL WORDS
OF LIFE"
Acts 5:1 through 6:7

And when they had brought them, they set them before the

26

council. And the high priest questioned them, saying, "We strictly charged you not to teach in this name, yet here you have filled Jerusalem with your teaching and you intend to bring this man's blood upon us." But Peter and the apostles answered, "We must obey God rather than men. The God of our fathers raised Jesus whom you killed by hanging him on a tree. God exalted him at his right hand as Leader and Savior, to give repentance to Israel and forgiveness of sins. And we are witnesses to these things, and so is the Holy Spirit whom God has given to those who obey him." (Acts 5:27-32)

Acts 5:17-21 tells of the second arrest and jailing of Peter and John by order of the chief priest. But within hours an angel of the Lord opened the prison doors and freed them. The angel said to them, "Go and stand in the temple and speak to the people all the words of this Life." (Acts 5:20)

Eventually Peter and John were brought before the Sanhedrin again. Peter again said, "We must obey God rather than men." (Acts 5:29) Gamaliel, a Pharisee himself, came to the apostles' rescue. He said:

". . . keep away from these men and let them alone; for if this plan or this undertaking is of men, it will fail; but if it is of God, you will not be able to overthrow them. You might even be found opposing God!" (Acts 5:38-39)

The council followed Gamaliel's advice. "Then they [apostles] left the presence of the council, rejoicing. . . ." (Acts 5:41) With this advice Gamaliel displayed an attitude that John Wesley also had. The attitude is one of tolerance and openness. Wesley was open to a wide diversity of opinion and belief within the church. He was willing that men who did not believe *just* as he believed remain in the church. He did not make a rigid adherence to one creed or code the test of a man's faith in God. This spirit of tolerance is a spirit the church needs today.

Acts 6:1-7 throws further light on the communal life of the early Christians. As in most groups, prejudices broke out against certain minorities. Acts 6:1 refers to "the Hellenists" who "murmured against the Hebrews because their widows were neglected in the daily distribution."

The Hellenists were Jews, newly converted to Christianity. They lived normally in Greek-speaking countries. They practiced Greek habits and customs. One ancient name for Greece was *Hellas*. Thus the term *Hellenists* refers to Jews who lived outside Palestine. They considered themselves to be pure Jewish stock. They looked upon Jerusalem as the center of their religion. So they had come to Jeru-

This impression of the healing of the beggar is very different from the drawing on page 25.

Albrecht Durer
Sts. Peter and John Healing at the Temple Gate
Yale University Art Gallery, Gift of Frederic George Achelis

salem for the Jewish festival of Pentecost. There they associated with the Jews of Judea, who were racial and religious purists.

The Hebrews (Acts 6:1) were Samaritans. In their literature the Samaritans referred to themselves as "Hebrews," not as "Jews." Judean Jews, as well as Hellenist Jews, also maintained this use of the word *Hebrew*. The Judean Jews and the Hellenist Jews considered the Samaritans racially and religiously impure. The impurity of the Samaritans dated from 721 B.C. In that year, Assyria captured Samaria. Tens of thousands of Samaritans were taken captive to Assyria. The Assyrians forced thousands of foreign captives to move to Samaria. Through marriage with these captives, the Samaritans soon had a mixed race, a mixed language, and a mixed religion. (Find Samaria on the map on page 41.)

Following the advice of Nehemiah and Ezra, the Jews of Judea had not married into the mixed race of Samaria. The Judean Jew was racially pure and obedient to the law of Moses.

In Jerusalem, Hebrews (Samaritans) and Hellenist Jews worshiped in one synagogue ("the synagogue of the Freedmen," Acts 6:9). Luke states that converts to Christ came from both groups—Hebrews (Samaritans) and Hellenist Jews. Both were minority groups in Jerusalem. Conflict was inevitable. Both groups felt mistreated. They claimed that their widows were neglected. Charges of partiality followed distrust.

So the apostles appointed "seven men of good repute, full of the Spirit and of wisdom" to "serve tables." Serving tables could mean (1) serving meals or (2) distributing money at the money tables. The new administrative group probably fulfilled both functions. With justice love can prosper.

The first major part of Luke's book ends with Acts 6:7. This part tells how the church was established in Jerusalem. Luke's final verse for this part is "And the word of God increased; and the number of the disciples multiplied greatly in Jerusalem, and a great many of the priests were obedient to the faith." (Acts 6:7) This passage says that even some of the priests were converted. These men found in Jesus, the Messiah, the ultimate authority in the kingdom of God.

4. One Covenant People
(*Acts 6:8 through 8:3*)

Luke wanted the "lovers of God" (Theophilus) to know how far Christianity had spread. In Acts 1:1 through 6:7 he told how the number of disciples increased in Jerusalem. Acts 6:7 ends the first major section of his book.

Luke also wanted his readers to know that the church spread through all Judea and Galilee and Samaria. So we find in Acts 6:8 through 9:31 Luke's second major section. This section is Luke's account of how the church expanded in Palestine beyond Jerusalem. Luke included in this story only records that would help his readers see that the call of Christ is to all men.

Luke knew Jewish Christians (such as Peter, John, and James), black Jewish Christians (such as the Ethiopian eunuch), Greek Christians (such as Timothy, Apollos, and Priscilla), and Hebrew (Samaritan) Christians (such as Stephen). Luke purposely included these varied types of "sons of the covenant." He meant to show how the faith spread from Jews in Jerusalem to Gentiles all over the world.

This lesson is about Stephen, the first Christian martyr. Stephen was probably a Samaritan who had been converted to Christianity. Samaritans were hated by Jews. Why did Luke include in Acts this account of a Christian who was a hated and inferior Samaritan? At his trial Stephen had the face of an angel. At his death he prayed for his enemies as Jesus prayed. Others could see the Holy Spirit in him. Luke wanted to show us that through a lowly Samaritan like Stephen men found Christ.

Read Acts 6:1 through 8:3 in your Bible before reading further in this chapter. Our conclusion in this lesson that Stephen was a Samaritan is based on ideas in *The Anchor Bible,* Volume 31, The Acts of the Apostles (Doubleday, 1967), pages 285-300. Most commentaries offer another point of view, saying that Stephen was a Hellenist.

A MAN FULL OF GRACE AND POWER
Acts 6:8-10

And Stephen, full of grace and power, did great wonders and signs among the people. Then some of those who belonged to the synagogue of the Freedmen (as it was called) . . . arose and disputed with Stephen. But they could not withstand the wisdom and the Spirit with which he spoke.

Let us think about Stephen's Samaritan background. We see three kinds of Christians in Acts 6:1-2. (1) The apostles and original disciples in Jerusalem were "Jews." They did not call themselves "Hebrews." (2) Christians who did call themselves "Hebrews" were Samaritans. Jews considered Samaritans inferior. For example, Samaritans were barred from the temple in Jerusalem. (3) Hellenistic Christians were converted Jews who lived normally outside Palestine. They were from cities such as Ephesus and Alexandria. They spoke Greek and were deeply influenced by Greek culture.

Stephen was a Hebrew (Samaritan). He was one of seven persons chosen to see that the widows of the Hellenists and Samaritans were treated fairly in the dole of money and food. (See Acts 6:1-6.)

Stephen's use of the Scriptures in his speech before the high priest shows us that he probably was a Samaritan. As we shall see later, his biblical quotations were from the Samaritan version of the Pentateuch (the first five books of the Old Testament). In his speech he did not quote the Jewish Bible but the Samaritan Bible.

Does it really matter whether Stephen used the Samaritan Bible or the Jewish Bible? Yes, it matters for several reasons. (1) Because Stephen used the Samaritan Bible, he was limited to the first five books of the Old Testament. The Samaritans did not regard the prophetic books as Scripture. (2) This limited his biblical understanding of the Messiah to ideas from the Samaritan Pentateuch. (3) Stephen's use of the Samaritan Bible explains some inconsistencies that a careful reader may notice in his speech before the high priest.

When one reads Acts 7:14-16, he may be puzzled. Here are two examples of apparent inconsistencies.

(1) Stephen says that seventy-five souls went down to Egypt with Jacob. (Acts 7:14) But Genesis 46:27 tells of seventy persons, not seventy-five.

(2) Stephen says that Jacob was buried in a tomb near Shechem. (Acts 7:16) But Genesis says he was buried near Hebron. (See both Genesis 23 and Genesis 50:1-14.) Shechem was the holy city of the Samaritans. They viewed Shechem in much the same way the Jews viewed Jerusalem. Stephen assumes that Abraham and Isaac are also buried near the Samaritan holy place. This again is inconsistent with the Jewish version of Genesis, which is the version we use today.

Scholars find many other inconsistencies. These inconsistencies suggest that Stephen was pitting the Samaritan view of history against the Jewish view. Stephen used his own Bible. And in doing so he shows us that he was a Samaritan.

Fortunately, Jesus' new covenant was offered to both Jew and

Which figure do you think is Paul?

Stephen Stoned to Death, by Paul Gustave Dore
Photo from Three Lions

Samaritan. Both groups looked to Abraham, Isaac, Jacob, and Joseph as "our fathers." Both looked forward to a coming Messiah, though each interpreted him according to the books of Scripture they accepted as valid. The early church was gracious enough to embrace Jews, Samaritans, and Hellenists. The love of God created a church that has room for *all* varieties of men.

THREE CHARGES AGAINST STEPHEN
Acts 6:11-15

"We have heard him speak blasphemous words against Moses and God." . . . **"This man never ceases to speak words against this holy place [the temple] and the law; for we have heard him say that this Jesus of Nazareth will destroy this place, and will change the customs which Moses delivered to us." (Acts 6:11, 13-14)**

In his ministry Stephen had to overcome three handicaps. (1) He was a Samaritan. (2) Being a Samaritan, he could not enter the temple area in Jerusalem to worship. (3) Samaritans were a mixed race. (See page 28.) Yet Stephen, a Samaritan, became a leader of the early Christian church. He reasoned and spoke well. He did signs and wonders, that is, miracles. No one could withstand his wisdom and spirit.

Serious charges and false witnesses were brought against Stephen. His accusers brought him to the Sanhedrin and placed three charges against him. They were these: (1) He utters "blasphemous words against Moses and God." (Acts 6: 11) (2) He speaks "words against this holy place [the Jerusalem temple] and the law." (Acts 6:13) (3) He claims that "Jesus of Nazareth will destroy this place, and will change the customs which Moses delivered to us." (Acts 6:14)

Luke paints a vivid word picture of Stephen before the Sanhedrin. The accusers are angry. So are the members of the Sanhedrin. Yet Stephen is calm and poised. "And gazing at him, all who sat in the council [Sanhedrin] saw that his face was like the face of an angel." (Acts 6:15) This is quite a characterization for a lowly Samaritan.

The high priest asked about the three charges, "Is this so?" In answer, Stephen gave a long speech. (Acts 7:2-53) Some scholars think that Luke may have copied this speech directly from a missionary tract that Stephen wrote to convert Samaritans.

We turn now to Stephen's defense. (Acts 7:2-53) We can divide this defense into four parts, as they stand in the Bible. Here we will discuss each part of the speech separately.

STEPHEN'S DEFENSE

Read Acts 7:2-8, where Stephen speaks of Abraham's covenant of circumcision.

> **"Brethren and fathers, hear me. The God of glory appeared to our father Abraham, when he was in Mesopotamia, before he lived in Haran. . . . And he [God] gave him the covenant of circumcision. . . ." (Acts 7:2, 8)**

What a way to begin a defense! Stephen began by affirming a faith in the covenant made between God and Abraham. Jews and Samaritans shared this faith. This Samaritan Christian argued that many beliefs unite Jews and Samaritans. At the same time, he spoke plainly about his own beliefs. For example, in that opening sentence he was true to his Samaritan Bible. He said that God appeared to Abraham while he was in Mesopotamia. Each Jew in the Sanhedrin would have shaken his head immediately and said, "No, God appeared to Abraham in Haran *after* he left Mesopotamia." (See Genesis 11:31 through 12:3.) We must admire Stephen's courage in saying what he had heard and read and believed.

The leaders in the Sanhedrin would have agreed with Stephen's reference to the covenant of circumcision. (Acts 7:8) But later he struck a prophetic blow. He said: You may have the physical mark of the covenant (circumcision) on your bodies, but you do not have the mental and spiritual marks of the covenant in your hearts. You are uncircumcised inwardly, in heart. (See Acts 7:51 and compare Romans 2:25-29.) This charge could have had only one effect. The Sanhedrin was enraged.

Stephen made a further point. The ancestors of the Samaritans and the ancestors of the Jews were formerly *one covenant people*. Abraham was their common father. "We Samaritans and Jews have a bond through the covenant that should unite, not divide," Stephen taught.

Read Acts 7:9-29, where Stephen says that God was with Joseph and Moses.

> And the patriarchs, jealous of Joseph, sold him into Egypt; but God was with him. . . . (Acts 7:9)

Stephen denied he blasphemed God. To the contrary: (1) He believed that God is a self-revealing God. (2) He believed that God reveals himself to covenant people *wherever they are*. Abraham was in Mesopotamia. (Acts 7:2) Joseph was in Egypt. (Acts 7:9) Moses was in Midian. (Acts 7:29-32) Joshua was in Samaria. (Acts 7:45) But God revealed himself to each of them. (3) He believed that God promises his presence to each son of the covenant. God will maintain his part in the covenant. *Emmanuel.* He is with us. This was not blasphemy. It was testimony! Stephen believed that God was with him too. He expressed this belief supremely when he faced death and saw heaven open before him and Jesus standing at the right hand of God.

Read Acts 7:30-37, where Stephen says a prophet greater than Moses has come.

> "Now when forty years had passed, an angel appeared to him [Moses] in the wilderness of Mount Sinai, in a flame of fire in a bush. . . . This is the Moses who said to the Israelites, 'God will raise up for you a prophet from your brethren as he raised me up.' " (Acts 7:30, 37)

Read Acts 7:37-43.

Every member of the Sanhedrin had prayed for the coming of the prophet who would be greater than Moses. (See Deuteronomy 18:15 and compare Acts 7:37.) Such a prophet—even a Messiah—had come in Jesus. But none of the Sanhedrin believed it. They prayed for a Messiah, but they did not believe their prayer had been answered.

Read Acts 7:44-53, where Stephen tells how Joshua brought the tent of witness to Shechem.

> "Our fathers had the tent of witness in the wilderness, even as he who spoke to Moses directed him to make it, according to the pattern that he had seen. Our fathers in turn brought it in with Joshua when they dispossessed the nations which God thrust out before our fathers. . . . . But it was Solomon who built a house for him. Yet the Most High does not dwell in houses made with hands. . . ." (Acts 7:44-45, 47-48)

The worship of God cannot be confined to one place. The temple in Jerusalem cannot be the only place where God is rightly worshiped. God's people are a pilgrim people. As the pilgrims move on, God moves with them. The worship and presence of God cannot be localized.

In other words, Stephen agreed with an insight Jesus expressed. Jesus was talking with a woman of Samaria, who said, "Our fathers worshiped on this mountain [Mount Gerizim near Shechem]; and you [Jews] say that in Jerusalem is the place where men ought to worship." Jesus answered: "Woman, believe me, the hour is coming when neither on this mountain nor in Jerusalem will you worship the Father. . . . God is spirit, and those who worship him must worship in spirit and truth." (John 4:20-21, 24)

Jesus and Stephen urged that men could find God in places other than the temple. Stephen had shown already that Abraham, Joseph, Moses, and Joshua found God outside Judea and without the temple. Jeremiah also, in his famous temple address (Jeremiah 7), said the Jews thought too much of their temple. They thought that just because they had the Lord's temple he would not bring his judgment against the city of Jerusalem. Instead of obedience to God, loyalty to the temple was their source of strength.

Stephen believed that the Sanhedrin elders were more dedicated to the temple than to spiritual worship. He remembered that Jesus had said the time would come when men would worship in places other than the temple. So he now attacked! His offense was razor sharp: "You stiff-necked people, uncircumcised in heart and ears, you always resist the Holy Spirit. As your fathers did, so do you." (Acts 7:51)

The Jews were the people of God's promises. God had made a covenant with their fathers and with them. They knew the challenge and promise expressed in Exodus 19:6: "You shall be to me a kingdom of priests and a holy nation." But Stephen said that they had not fulfilled that calling. They carried the sign of the covenant (circumcision) on their bodies. But they did not have the grace of the covenant in their hearts. Their motives and attitudes were uncircumcised. They refused to listen to the Holy Spirit. Their ears heard that Jesus is the resurrected Christ, the fulfillment of the covenant of the patriarchs. Jesus is the prophet greater than Moses whom they all expected. They heard that God's Spirit had come with the risen Lord. Stephen told them they should respond to God by repenting for their refusals to answer His call.

Even today, the risen Christ calls for new men, men whose minds and motives are marked by his Spirit.

STEPHEN AFFIRMS THE AUTHORITY OF JESUS
Acts 7:54 through 8:3

> **Now when they heard these things they were enraged, and they ground their teeth against him. . . . and he said, "Behold, I see the heavens opened, and the Son of man standing at the right hand of God." (Acts 7:54-56)**

They considered Stephen's claim that Jesus was next to God in authority to be blasphemy. So they killed him. Stephen's execution was not a legal act because the Sanhedrin did not have the authority to condemn a man to death or to execute him. In uncontrolled anger the religious leaders of Judea "cast him out of the city" into a pit (as was the custom) and cast stones upon him.

> **Then they cast him out of the city and stoned him; and the witnesses laid down their garments at the feet of a young man named Saul. And as they were stoning Stephen, he prayed, "Lord Jesus, receive my spirit." And he knelt down and cried with a loud voice, "Lord, do not hold this sin against them." And when he had said this, he fell asleep. And Saul was consenting to his death. (Acts 7:58 through 8:1a)**

The Samaritan Christian Stephen witnessed to his Lord with his last breath. He prayed that God would forgive his enemies. He gave his spirit into the keeping of the risen Christ who waited for him. He died loyal to his faith that God loved him.

Read the end of this story in Acts 8:1b-3. The Samaritan Christians scattered, though the Jewish Christians apparently stayed in Jerusalem. Saul was concerned about the purity of the Jewish faith. So he set about imprisoning as many of the followers of Christ as he could. But Saul's memory of the way the Samaritan died may well have been what caused him to question his ideals of doctrinal and ritual purity. His memory of Stephen was a great and terrible thing. Augustine said that the church owes Paul to the prayer of Stephen. Whose life do our prayers and actions win to Christ?

5. A Church for the Outcasts
(Acts 8:4 through 9:31)

This lesson shows the risen Lord's concern for men whom others considered undesirable. The Scripture for this lesson mentions three outcast groups: (1) Samaritans, (2) eunuchs, (3) enemies. Read Acts 8:4 through 9:31 in your Bible now.

Our Scripture deals with the work of two Christian men—Philip and Paul. After Stephen's death, Christians who were not Judeans were persecuted. Samaritan Christians and Hellenist Christians fled to their homelands. The "seven" who waited tables for the Hellenist and Hebrew widows were forced to leave Jerusalem. Among them was Philip. Philip probably witnessed Paul's approval of Stephen's death. Paul's conversion to Stephen's Christ led to the planting of Christianity in Europe. We shall divide the Scripture for this lesson into two parts. First we will study Philip. Then we will study Paul.

PHILIP'S MESSAGE
Acts 8:4-8

> Now those who were scattered went about preaching the word. Philip went down to a city of Samaria, and proclaimed to them the Christ. (Acts 8:4-5)

Acts 8:4-8 describes Philip's reaction to persecution. He did not sulk or moan about his fate. He may have felt that he should carry on the work that Stephen had begun in Samaria. So Philip went to the Samaritans.

We must remember that the Samaritans recognized only the first five books of the Old Testament as Scripture. The Samaritan version of the Pentateuch was a very limited "Bible" for preaching that Jesus was the Messiah. Tradition says that Philip went to Gitta, a city west of the capital of Samaria. There he preached to the Samaritans. Remember that the Jews of Jerusalem considered the Samaritans unworthy to worship in the temple of the Holy City. Philip knew the sense of inferiority this attitude created. He knew the anger and resentment that can come from such an attitude. He saw Stephen wince under the verbal lash of thoughtlessness and unkindness. He probably saw Stephen die.

Philip's message was threefold. (1) Men can become new creatures as they accept Christ. ("Unclean spirits came out of many who were possessed." Acts 8:7) (2) There is healing for the sick, lame, and paralyzed. ("Many who were paralyzed or lame were healed." Acts 8:7) (3) When the body and mind are healed happiness and joy follow. Philip's enthusiastic faith was contagious, for "there was much joy in that city." (Acts 8:8) What a compliment to a man who was forced to leave Jerusalem as an undesirable heretic. Philip's preaching led to harmony, healing, and joy, all signs that the Messiah has come.

IN THE DAYS OF PISCES AND AQUARIUS
Acts 8:9-25

How similar our day and Philip's day are in some ways. Astrologers gave readings to thousands of clients. Big business "deals" were concluded only when the signs were right. The date of one's birth was watched carefully to note the influence of Pisces and Aquarius (or others) on one's destiny.

> But there was a man named Simon who had previously practiced magic in the city and amazed the nation of Samaria, saying that he himself was somebody great. They all gave heed to him, from the least to the greatest, saying, "This man is that power of God which is called Great." . . . Even Simon himself believed, and after being baptized he continued with Philip. (Acts 8:9-10, 13)

This passage (Acts 8:9-25) tells of Simon, a resident of Gitta. He was a "magus," a magician and astrologer. He had awed the Samaritans with his magical arts. He was regarded as a god, even in his own day. As late as the second century, many Samaritans still considered Simon divine. He thought that the planets determine our fate and destiny. But he was more than an astrologer. He later was known as the father of gnosticism, a heresy of the early church.

"Even Simon himself believed, and after being baptized he continued with Philip." (Acts 8:13) Simon had found Christ. His conversion may have been sincere. But later events show how incomplete it was. We suspect that Philip was not quite sure what to do with this magus. But when Peter and John came to Samaria something happened that called for Simon to make a decision.

The two figures in the cloud represent God the Father and Christ the Son.

The Conversion of St. Paul, by Luca Cambiaso
The Art Museum, Princeton University

> Now when Simon saw that the Spirit was given through the laying
> on of the apostles' hands, he offered them money, saying, "Give
> me also this power, that any one on whom I lay my hands may
> receive the Holy Spirit." (Acts 8:18-19)

Simon wanted to buy the power to impart the Spirit. He must have
viewed Peter as a super-magician. But Simon overlooked the character of the apostles, who laid their hands on the heads of believers.
Character, faith, and spiritual power cannot be purchased. To this
day the word *simony* refers to the attempt to buy spiritual power
with money. Simon was not interested in helping people to experience
the presence of the Holy Spirit. He wanted prestige and power.

I watched an Eastern Orthodox priest in Belgrade lay his hands
on the heads of the faithful after a Sunday service. As they knelt
before him, he placed his hands on their heads. He unhurriedly
prayed briefly over each person and crossed each person's forehead
with oil. The faithful rose with glory in their faces. They were ready
to move out into their Communist land, a land ruled by unbelievers.
You cannot buy that kind of power.

OUTCASTS OF THE RELIGIOUS INSTITUTION
Acts 8:26-40

> But an angel of the Lord said to Philip, "Rise and go toward
> the south to the road that goes down from Jerusalem to Gaza."
> This is a desert road. And he rose and went. And behold, an
> Ethiopian, a eunuch . . . was reading the prophet Isaiah . . . .
> Then Philip opened his mouth, and beginning with this scripture
> he told him the good news of Jesus. (Acts 8:26-27, 28, 35)

What did Philip, Stephen, the woman at the well, and the Ethiopian
have in common? They were all considered outcasts. The Jews
thought them unworthy to worship in the temple at Jerusalem. Samaritans were a mixed race. They had mixed moral and religious
standards. The Ethiopian was a black eunuch. A eunuch could not
enter the temple. (See Deuteronomy 23:1, Leviticus 21:20 and
22:24.) He could not be part of a Jewish congregation. Philip had
just completed a ministry to the Samaritans. He would not have
despised an Ethiopian (black man). The black man had been to
Jerusalem to worship. This would have been an expensive experience.
He came all the way from Ethiopia to Jerusalem. And he would
have found he could not enter the temple after he got there. So his
mind must have been full of questions. Why shouldn't he be admitted?
What kind of God would keep out certain kinds of people? Isn't
God interested in all nations and in all kinds of people, including
eunuchs?

5. A CHURCH FOR THE OUTCASTS

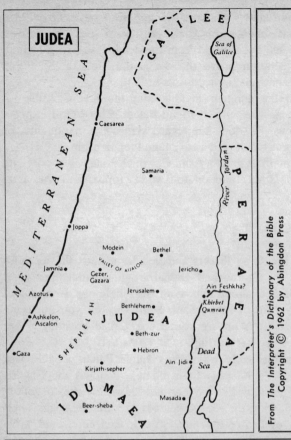

From The Interpreter's Dictionary of the Bible
Copyright © 1962 by Abingdon Press

This lesson mentions Samaria, Gaza, Azotus, Joppa, and Caesarea. This map shows their location. The area shown in this map is in modern Israel.

Recall that he was reading Isaiah 53 when Philip came up. Just three chapters ahead he might also have read:

> **"For thus says the Lord:**
> **'To the eunuchs who keep my sabbaths,**
> **who choose the things that please me**
> **and hold fast my covenant . . .**
> **I will give them an everlasting name**
> **which shall not be cut off.' " (Isaiah 56:4-5)**

Philip's sensitivities cried out in the eunuch's behalf. At the black man's request, Philip got into the chariot and began to interpret Isaiah 53. He made two points. (1) In his suffering and death, Jesus

CHANNELS OF HIS SPIRIT

was similar to the "lamb" who opened not his mouth. Luke 23:9 tells that Jesus was dumb at his trial, refusing to speak in his own behalf. (2) Jesus had been raised from the dead. Jesus' resurrection, ascension, and exaltation prove that he is the Messiah. So Philip "told him the good news of Jesus." (Acts 8:35)

Philip baptized the eunuch, making him the first Christian of Northeastern Africa. The eunuch found that in Christ God is not a respecter of persons. He does not regard skin color, nationality, or physical handicaps as barriers to a covenantal relationship.

Philip then went to Azotus (Ashdod, which today is a port city of black Jews, in Israel) and on to Lydda, Joppa, and Caesarea, where he lived.

PAUL MEETS CHRIST
Acts 9:1-9

> But Saul, still breathing threats and murder against the disciples of the Lord, . . . approached Damascus, and suddenly a light from heaven flashed about him. And he fell to the ground and heard a voice saying to him, "Saul, Saul, why do you persecute me?" And he said, "Who are you, Lord?" And he said, "I am Jesus, whom you are persecuting. . . ." (Acts 9:1, 3-5)

Saul's full name probably was Gaius Julius Paulus. "Saul" was his Hebrew name, "Paulus" his Latin name. "Paul" is the English name. What did Paul look like? We do not know for sure. A collection of legends written in the second century says that he was a small man with meeting eyebrows, a rather large hooked nose, bald, a bit bowlegged, strongly built, and "full of grace." He was a Roman citizen. He spoke Greek, Hebrew, and probably Latin. He probably attended the University of Tarsus before he went to the rabbinical school of Gamaliel in Jerusalem.

Paul was loyal to the law, as his teacher Gamaliel interpreted it to him in Jerusalem. As a Pharisee, he believed that a man is saved only by obedience to the law, by carefully observing all the written and unwritten traditions of the law. His persecuting zeal for the law was similar to the zeal of Elijah, who called for vengeance on the enemies of God. (1 Kings 18:36-40)

Like many of his forefathers, Paul "breathed threats and murder" against those who did not think as he did. Hating Christians, he sought those "belonging to the Way" in order to arrest them. In fulfilling his zeal he witnessed and approved the murder of Stephen. But he always remembered that Stephen died with a prayer of forgiveness for Paul and his other enemies and with an awareness of the presence of the risen Lord. On the road to Damascus, Paul too experienced the presence of Christ. (Read all of Acts 9:1-31.)

You should also read all of the three passages that describe Paul's conversion. They are Acts 9:3-19; 22:3-16; 26:9-18. Each varies a bit from the others, but all have the same key point. Christ revealed himself to Paul. Paul found the Messiah. Christ converted Paul through a vision and called him to a special mission.

You may find it strange that the first revelation of Christ outside Palestine was to the worst persecutor. How did it occur? What happened?

We should begin with the simple fact that this was Paul's religious experience. The group of men with him shared the experience only in part. Acts 9:7 says that those traveling with Paul heard the voice but saw no one. Acts 22:9 says they saw the light but did not hear the voice. The details of the story vary, but the heart of the matter is the same. Paul saw the light. Paul heard Jesus speak. Paul received a new vocation. He became God's agent to evangelize the Gentiles.

What was the light? Fire and light are symbols for the presence of God. In this case the light is a symbol for the presence of the living Christ. "For it is the God who said, 'Let light shine out of darkness,' who has *shone in our hearts to give the light* of the knowledge of the glory of God in the face of Christ." (2 Corinthians 4:6, italics added)

When Paul experienced the light shining in his heart, he fell to the ground, as Moses had fallen on his face in God's presence. Immediately he heard the voice of the risen Christ, Jesus of Nazareth. What an experience! He had seen Jesus Christ.

Paul had been persecuting the church. But Jesus said, "Why do you persecute me?" Jesus identified with the church. If you persecute, make fun of, laugh at, or want to destroy the church, you do these things to Jesus Christ. Christ is present in the church and suffers when the church suffers.

Paul responded in several ways. (1) He was struck blind. "I could not see because of the brightness of that light." (Acts 22:11. See also Acts 9:8.) (2) He realized that Jesus is the Messiah and the Lord. He alone is the divine Savior, the one who saves. (3) Paul realized that the church is Jesus himself. (4) He was willing to learn more. He went to Damascus and waited to be told what to do. (Acts 9:6)

PAUL IN DAMASCUS
Acts 9:10-31

Now there was a disciple at Damascus named Ananias. The Lord said to him in a vision, "Ananias." And he said, "Here I am, Lord." . . . "Go, for he is a chosen instrument of mine to carry

> **my name before the Gentiles and kings and the sons of Israel. . . ."**
> **(Acts 9:10, 15)**

In this passage (Acts 9:10-19) Ananias obeyed Christ, who urged him to go to Paul and explain the faith to him. At first Ananias tried to correct Christ. (See Acts 9:13.) But finally he listened and allowed Christ to guide him. As he entered the house where Paul was, he said, "Brother Saul, the Lord Jesus . . . has sent me that you may regain your sight and be filled with the Holy Spirit." (Acts 9:17) What a way to greet a man he feared: "Brother Christian!" Paul regained his sight, both physically and spiritually.

The significance of Paul's conversion is basically threefold. (1) Jesus was alive. Paul now believed in His resurrection. Jesus the crucified is the living Messiah, the Son of God. (2) The truth He had learned is for all people of all nations. (3) Paul saw himself as the apostle to the Gentiles. He was to lead in a conquest of the world for Christ.

> **For several days he was with the disciples at Damascus. And in the synagogues immediately he proclaimed Jesus, saying, "He is the Son of God." (Acts 9:19-20)**

Paul states in Galatians 1:17-18 that he went to Arabia for three years at this time. This three-year period may be covered by Luke's phrase *for several days*. Paul needed to rethink his faith in quietness. Jesus spent forty days in the wilderness. How much more time would Paul need to reshape his thinking and reinterpret the Scriptures from a new point of view. He probably went to Petra, where King Aretas governed Idumea.

Later, Barnabas sponsored Paul for a brief visit in Jerusalem, where he conferred with the Twelve. He also "went in and out among them at Jerusalem, preaching boldly in the name of the Lord." (Acts 9:28-29) Apparently Paul spoke in the same synagogue where Stephen had been taken and murdered. This required courage. Yet, for fear of his own life, he had to leave Jerusalem for Caesarea. He went from there to Tarsus, his native city, where he remained for ten years.

Acts 9:31 is a summary statement that concludes the second section of Acts. This section tells of the expansion of the church throughout Palestine.

6. What God Has Cleansed
(Acts 9:32 through 11:18)

Luke wrote Acts in order to give Theophilus an account of the growth of Christianity. Luke divided Acts into six parts. We have studied two of these sections: (1) the church in Jerusalem and Peter's preaching (Acts 1:1 through 6:7) and (2) the expansion of the church through Palestine (Acts 6:8 through 9:31). We are ready to study the third section of Acts—the expansion of the church to Antioch (Acts 9:32 through 12:24).

Look at the last verse of each of these different sections. Part 1: "And the word of God increased; and the number of the disciples multiplied greatly in Jerusalem, and a great many of the priests were obedient to the faith." (Acts 6:7) Part 2: "So the church throughout all Judea and Galilee and Samaria had peace and was built up; and walking in the fear of the Lord and in the comfort of the Holy Spirit it was multiplied." (Acts 9:31) Part 3: "But the word of God grew and multiplied." (Acts 12:24) These three brief summaries show that expansion and growth are keynotes in Acts.

This lesson is the first of two lessons on the third part of Acts. This part deals with Peter's ministries at Lydda, Joppa, and Caesarea. (Acts 9:32 through 11:18)

Read Acts 9:32 through 11:18 in your Bible before reading further in this Student Book.

PETER'S MINISTRIES AT LYDDA AND JOPPA
Acts 9:32-43

Now as Peter went here and there among them all, he came down also to the saints that lived at Lydda. There he found a man named Aeneas, who had been bedridden for eight years and was paralyzed. And Peter said to him, "Aeneas, Jesus Christ heals you...." And immediately he rose. (Acts 9:32-34)

The apostle Peter seems to have been a kind of "presiding elder." He went from charge to charge to see how the work was progressing.

45

We recall how Philip worked in Samaria, converting many. Luke reports, "Now when the apostles at Jerusalem heard that Samaria had received the word of God, they sent to them Peter and John, who came down and prayed for them that they might receive the Holy Spirit." (Acts 8:14-15) With the same concerns, Peter follows again in Philip's footsteps in the west. After Philip had baptized the Ethiopian eunuch, he went to Azotus. And then "passing on he preached the gospel to all the towns till he came to Caesarea." (Acts 8:40) This meant that Philip preached at Lydda, Joppa, and in the small villages of Sharon. (Sharon was the name for the coastal plain along the Mediterranean Sea. Joppa was on the coast thirty-five miles from Jerusalem. Lydda was eleven miles southeast of Joppa.)

Peter traveled the road Philip had traveled. His concern was to confirm the new Christians in those places where Philip had preached.

At Lydda Peter healed Aeneas, and of course he witnessed to his faith there. Soon "all the residents of Lydda and Sharon saw him, and they turned to the Lord." (Acts 9:35) Then Peter went on to Joppa to visit another city where Philip had witnessed.

Now there was at Joppa a disciple named Tabitha, which means Dorcas. She was full of good works and acts of charity. In those days she fell sick and died. . . . (Acts 9:36-37)

Tabitha worked with a number of widows (Acts 9:39) who were committed to helping the poor. They did "good works and acts

Christ between Saint Peter and Saint James Major
Attributed to Cimabue
National Gallery of Art, Washington, D. C.
Andrew Mellon Collection

This Saint James is the son of Zebedee. The Latin words mean I am the Light of the World.

of charity." (Acts 9:36) After she died, her friends called Peter from Lydda. They displayed many garments she had made to give to the needy. Peter was deeply touched by her obvious kindness and love. After requesting all the mourners to leave the room, Peter knelt and prayed for Tabitha. His prayer shows that he knew that healing power belongs to God. Peter knew that he had no power over life and death in his own hands. His power lay in the hands of the Christlike God. The Father heard his prayer and restored Tabitha to life. (This story resembles the story of Jesus and the twelve-year-old girl in Mark 5:38-42. The resemblance tells us that the healing ministry of Jesus was continued by his church.)

Peter called the "saints and widows" and presented Tabitha alive to them. The word *saint* is an important word in the New Testament. It refers to "holy ones" in the sense that saints are different from other people. They are different because they are called by Christ to a new life. They respond affirmatively to that call. Life for them is more than making and saving money and possessions. Life is primarily spiritual. Life is choosing the spiritual values that express kindness, love, compassion, justice, loyalty to God's purposes.

When the Old Testament refers to "saints," it means the chosen people, Israel. For Peter a saint is one who responds to the call of the risen Christ. A saint is one who has experienced the presence of the Holy Spirit in his life. His actions are motivated by the values that guided Christ—love, joy, compassion, justice, loyalty to God. Such "separated ones" (saints) are the true holy ones of Israel.

Luke reports that two disciples from Joppa went to Lydda to get Peter. These disciples were possibly converts of Philip's ministry. After the healing of Tabitha (Dorcas), Peter went to the home of one of these disciples, Simon, a tanner. A tanner had about the lowest job a Jew could take. Because he worked with skins of various animals, he and his family were unclean and off limits to Jews. But this is the very type of person to whom Philip went. Philip's ministry was to unwanted and undesirable people, such as Samaritans and eunuchs.

Peter stayed at the place recommended by the "saints and widows" of Joppa. (See Acts 9:41.) The saints looked not at the work the tanner did, but at his heart, as Philip had done. Peter, "the presiding elder," was housed with the lowliest of Joppa—Simon, the tanner. This fact may have led him to thoughts about clean and unclean persons.

A SOLDIER OF OCCUPATION SEEKS CHRIST
Acts 10:1-8

At Caesarea there was a man named Cornelius, a centurion of what was known as the Italian Cohort, a devout man who feared God with all his household, gave alms liberally to the people, and prayed constantly to God. (Acts 10:1-2)

Caesarea was a city on the coast of the Mediterranean Sea. It was a grand and beautiful harbor city built by Herod the Great in honor of the Emperor Caesar Augustus. It was the administrative capital of Judea. Pilate had lived here. It was also the headquarters for the occupying Roman army.

Caesarea was the city where Philip the evangelist lived. (Acts 21:8) He had four daughters who prophesied, too. His was quite a family. Philip, by nature and calling, would have witnessed to whoever would listen in his hometown. Perhaps he had spoken to Cornelius.

Cornelius was an officer of the Roman army of occupation, stationed in Caesarea. He might have heard Philip and his daughters witness. As a soldier Cornelius knew courage and loyalty. From his travels as a centurion (a man who commanded a hundred soldiers), he had observed various religious claims and customs. He found none to satisfy him. He did believe in one God, as the Jews claimed. And he worshiped in their synagogue. He gave alms to the Jewish needy, and he prayed to the Lord. He was called a "God-fearer," a title given to non-Jews who worshiped the Lord but did not become Jews. That is, they were not circumcised. They did not accept all the laws of Judaism. Cornelius was the kind of man who yearns to hear about Christ. Our Scripture assumes that he knew something about Jesus.

"About the ninth hour of the day [3:00 P.M.] he saw clearly in a vision an angel of God coming in and saying to him, 'Cornelius.' And he stared at him in terror, and said, 'What is it, Lord?'" (Acts 10:3-4) Christ was speaking through the "angel" to Cornelius. He told him to send for Peter at Joppa, who was staying at the house of Simon, the tanner.

The Greek word *angelos* means "messenger." *Messenger* may be interpreted in either of two ways. (1) The messenger may be supernatural. (2) The messenger may be mortal. The word *angelos* may have either meaning. Sometimes the two meanings refer to the same person. A mortal man may do angelic things. I can imagine needy persons saying of Tabitha's gifts, "What an angel she is!" Have you ever said that about a person who has helped you when you were ill? A person may look like an angel. When Stephen was on trial, "his face was like the face of an angel." (Acts 6:15) That is, he had the look of a messenger of God. Cornelius himself gives an example of this identification of a man as an angel. (Acts 10:30-31) He told Peter how he had been at prayer, when "a *man* stood before me in bright apparel, saying, 'Cornelius, your prayer has been heard. . . .' " The angel who spoke to Cornelius may have been a human being, perhaps even Philip. The angel may have been a supernatural being. Whoever that angel was, Christ was speaking through him to the heart of Cornelius.

PETER'S OPENNESS
Acts 10:9-24

Peter went up on the housetop to pray, about the sixth hour. And he became hungry and desired something to eat; but while they were preparing it, he fell into a trance and saw the heaven opened. . . . (Acts 10:9-11)

Cornelius sent two soldiers and a slave to look for Peter at Simon's house. Just before they arrived, Peter was praying. His prayer was affected by the fact that he was hungry. His prayer may also have been affected by the "unclean" house where he was eating and sleeping. What attitudes should a Christian Jew have in a tanner's house? Was Peter himself ritually unclean? What does God call unclean anyway?

Loving his Scriptures, Peter probably recalled Genesis 1. Genesis 1 says that everything God made was good. After making all the animals, including pigs, God said, "It is good." After creating mankind, God said, "It is good." If God said all creation is good, how can man deny God's evaluation? Who can say that certain animals and certain men are unclean? Is Simon's house unacceptable (unclean) simply because he tans animal hides? Is the tanner himself unclean? Should Jews not associate with him?

Peter probably also recalled the debate between Jesus and some Pharisees about what is clean and what is unclean. Jesus told some Pharisees that the food a person eats does not defile him. It is what enters the heart of a man that defiles him. The "heart" is where motives and attitudes grow. Jesus said, " 'Do you not see that whatever goes into a man from outside cannot defile him, since it enters, not his heart but his stomach, and so passes on?' (Thus he declared

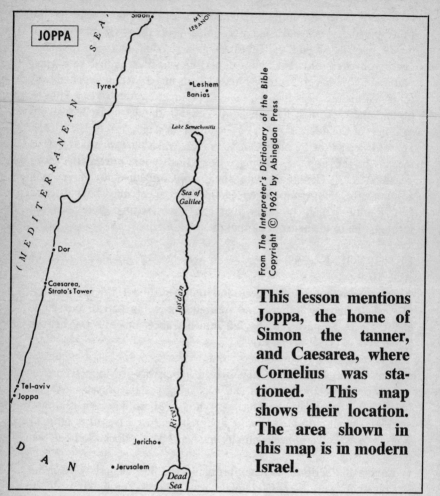

JOPPA

From The Interpreter's Dictionary of the Bible
Copyright © 1962 by Abingdon Press

This lesson mentions Joppa, the home of Simon the tanner, and Caesarea, where Cornelius was stationed. This map shows their location. The area shown in this map is in modern Israel.

all foods clean.) And he said, 'What comes out of man is what defiles a man. For from within, out of the heart of man, come evil thoughts, fornication, theft, murder, adultery, coveting, wickedness, deceit, licentiousness, envy, slander, pride, foolishness. All these evil things come from within, and they defile a man.'" (Mark 7:18-23) A man's thinking (heart) is what may defile him.

What is the real issue? May I eat ham? May I eat beef on Fridays? Should I abstain from certain foods (like candy) during Lent? These questions are irrelevant. They have little to do with the spiritual life. What you think about is the real issue. How should a Christian Jew think about a tanner (Simon), or a soldier of occupation (Cornelius), or a person of another race (the Ethiopian)? Attitudes are the real issue, not food, clothing, race, or vocation.

Peter's thoughts crystallized in a vision. In the vision he saw a huge cloth, like a sheet, slowly descend from heaven. In it were both clean and unclean animals. Peter, the Christian Jew, was hungry enough to eat a ham sandwich. But his early training at the synagogue in Capernaum was strong. "No, Lord; for I have never eaten anything that is common or unclean." And again the voice said, "What God has cleansed, you must not call common." (Acts 10:14, 15) Three times he heard this message. Then he saw the sheet, with its clean and unclean animals drawn up into heaven. Peter must have thought: Unclean things in the presence of God? Impossible, for God himself had called them good, and therefore clean. God made and is surrounded by only good and clean things.

> And while Peter was pondering the vision, the Spirit said to him, "Behold, three men are looking for you. Rise and go down, and accompany them without hesitation; for I have sent them." (Acts 10:19-20)

So the next day Peter, with a few disciples from Joppa and the servants from Cornelius, went to Caesarea. "Cornelius was expecting them and had called together his kinsmen and close friends." (Acts 10:24) Peter witnessed to them.

PETER'S WITNESS TO CORNELIUS
Acts 10:25-48

> You yourselves know how unlawful it is for a Jew to associate with or to visit any one of another nation, but God has shown me that I should not call any man common or unclean. So when I was sent for, I came without objection. I ask then why you sent for me. (Acts 10:28-29)

Peter began with half an apology. You know I'm doing something I shouldn't be doing. We Jews aren't supposed to socialize with non-Jews. But then Peter realized this problem was not one of socializing with people of another race. (He faced that problem later, at Antioch and at the Jerusalem Council. See Acts 15.) His concern at this time was to bring these Gentiles the good news of God's love as seen in Christ.

Cornelius explained to Peter about his need "to hear all that you have been commanded by the Lord." (Acts 10:33) Then Peter addressed them.

Read carefully Acts 10:34-43. This is Peter's summary of the gospel. It says more about the earthly career of Jesus than any other part of Acts. Several points stand out. (1) "God shows no partiality." Literally, "God is not a respecter of faces." God does not look to see skin color, shape of noses, or slant of eyes. (2) Jesus preached the good news (the Word) to Israel. It is now available to all mankind, for "Jesus is Lord of all." (3) Jesus of Nazareth was "anointed" (that is, made Messiah) at his baptism with the Holy Spirit and with power. (4) He went about doing good and healing all who were oppressed. (5) Jesus was put to death "by hanging him on a tree; but God raised him on the third day and made him manifest." He is the resurrected Lord. Peter says that he himself had seen the resurrected Lord. (6) Jesus Christ will judge the living and the dead. He knows what moves people. And on that basis will he judge their lives. (See Matthew 25:31-46.) (7) All who believe in him will receive forgiveness of sins through his name.

The household of Cornelius was willing to accept these claims from Christ. The risen Christ obviously desired to win them to his Kingdom. The Jews had received the Holy Spirit in Jerusalem. Now, in like manner, the Gentiles received the Spirit in Caesarea. This was the Gentile Pentecost. "The Holy Spirit fell on all who heard the word." (Acts 10:44) The disciples who had come from Joppa were amazed. But Peter commanded that they baptize the Gentiles "in the name of Jesus Christ."

PETER'S REPORT TO THE APOSTLES IN JERUSALEM
Acts 11:1-18

> So when Peter went up to Jerusalem, the circumcision party criticized him, saying, "Why did you go to uncircumcised men and eat with them?" But Peter began and explained to them in order: " . . . As I began to speak, the Holy Spirit fell on them just as on us at the beginning. And I remembered the word of the Lord, how he said, 'John baptized with water, but you shall be baptized with the Holy Spirit.' " (Acts 11:2-4, 15-16)

Peter told in Jerusalem about his witness to the Gentiles in Caesarea. And he told how the Holy Spirit came upon them. The baptism of the Holy Spirit is the authenticating experience. It is the work of the risen Lord himself. "When they [representatives of the circumcision party] heard this they were silenced. And they glorified God, saying, 'Then to the Gentiles also God has granted repentance unto life.' " (Acts 11:18)

The mission to the Gentiles had begun. It was to spread throughout the world, to such faraway places as North America and Russia. What unheard-of possibilities!

7. The Church at Antioch
(Acts 11:19 through 12:24)

The Acts of the Apostles tells how the gospel spread in Jerusalem and beyond. Philip carried the gospel to Samaria and to the coastal cities Joppa, Lydda, and Caesarea. The Word spread north to Phoenicia, Cyprus, and Antioch. Peter carried it to Cornelius the Gentile. Then Christians who fled from Jerusalem after Stephen's death carried the gospel to Antioch. (Antioch in Syria was three hundred miles north of Jerusalem.)

Read now Acts 11:19 through 12:24.

CHRIST HAILED AS LORD
Acts 11:19-20

> Now those who were scattered because of the persecution that arose over Stephen traveled as far as Phoenicia and Cyprus and Antioch, speaking the word to none except Jews. But there were some of them, men of Cyprus and Cyrene, who on coming to Antioch spoke to the Greeks also, preaching the Lord Jesus.

Two bands of Christians witnessed to their faith at Antioch. (1) Most of the scattered Christians spoke only to Jews in the synagogues. (2) A few Christians, "men of Cyprus and Cyrene, . . . spoke to the Greeks also." As soon as these men of Cyprus and Cyrene arrived in Antioch, they preached to the Greeks that Jesus is Lord.

Consider the city of Antioch. (1) Antioch was the capital of the Roman province of Syria. (2) It was one of the three largest cities of the Roman Empire. (3) Except perhaps for Corinth, Antioch was the most immoral city in the Roman world. The groves of Daphne, with their waterfalls, cypress trees, and lovely flower gardens, were dedicated to "sacred" prostitution. (4) Antioch was noted for its chariot racing, gambling, night clubs, drunkenness, and debauchery. (Note that two cities named Antioch are mentioned in Acts. One was in Syria. The other was in Pisidia, modern Turkey.)

Antioch seems to us a city where it would have been fruitless to preach the gospel. But the Christians from Cyprus and Cyrene disagreed. They preached to the Greeks. They did not go just to the synagogues to preach only to Jews.

The Greek cults taught that their gods were the lords of life. The men from Cyprus contradicted this claim. They stated boldly: (1) After a ministry of healing, loving, and redeeming persons, Jesus was killed. (2) God raised him from the dead. (3) This resurrected

53

Jesus is the one Lord of life. He rightly claims leadership over the spiritual life of mankind. Though many persons of Antioch scoffed, some found a Savior and a new life. Today Antioch is known as the city second only to Jerusalem in importance to the early church.

THE INFLUENCE OF A MAN OF ENCOURAGEMENT
Acts 11:21-26

And the hand of the Lord was with them, and a great number that believed turned to the Lord. News of this came to the ears of the church in Jerusalem, and they sent Barnabas to Antioch. . . . So Barnabas went to Tarsus to look for Saul; and when he had found him, he brought him to Antioch. (Acts 11:21-22, 25-26)

The church at Jerusalem sent Barnabas to check on the new mission in Antioch.

What do we know about Joseph Barnabas? (1) Luke calls him "the Son of encouragement." (Acts 4:36) He believed in people. For example, he introduced Paul to the church in Jerusalem after his conversion near Damascus. (See Acts 9:27.) (2) He came from a priestly family. He was a Levite and a native of Cyprus. (3) He was a generous and kind person. For example, he sold a field and gave the money to the apostles for the needs of the Christian fellowship. (4) Barnabas encouraged Paul to leave Tarsus to minister to the pagans in Antioch. (5) With Paul's help, Barnabas moved the center of the Christian movement from Jerusalem to Antioch. (6) He was "a good man, full of the Holy Spirit and of faith." (Acts 11:24)

Joseph Barnabas rejoiced over what he saw happening to the Greek Christians in Antioch. He saw a vast opening for Christian witness. So he went in search of Paul. He knew Paul's ability to persuade. He knew Paul's keen insight about Christ and God's plan for the Gentiles. He knew that Paul had a contagious faith.

Soon Paul was with Barnabas in Antioch. There they spent "a whole year . . . with the church, and taught a large company of people; and in Antioch the disciples were for the first time called Christians." (Acts 11:26)

The word *Christian* is the English version of a Latin word, *Christianus*. It means "one who belongs to or believes in Christ." Perhaps it was first used as a word of derision. It was similar to the modern title "Jesus freaks."

CONCERN FOR THE HUNGRY
Acts 11:27-30

Now in these days prophets came down from Jerusalem to Antioch. And one of them . . . foretold by the Spirit that there would

Photograph from Three Lions

be a great famine over all the world. . . . And the disciples
determined, every one according to his ability, to send relief to the
brethren who lived in Judea. . . . (Acts 11:27-29)

As you read this passage in your Bibles, you see that "prophets"
came from Jerusalem to Antioch. One of them was Agabus. Perhaps
you have questions about New Testament prophets. We recall many
Old Testament prophets, such as Isaiah, Jeremiah, and Ezekiel. The
New Testament prophet was born at Pentecost. Recall how Joel's
prophecy ("your sons and your daughters shall prophesy") was fulfilled at Pentecost. (See Acts 2:17.)

Any Christian may become a prophet. All Christians should seek
to prophesy. (See 1 Corinthians 14:1.) But some Christians have

greater prophetic gifts than others. These gifts of the Spirit include: (1) explaining prophetic Scriptures under the guidance of the Holy Spirit (see 1 Peter 1:10-12); (2) expounding the mystery of the divine plan (see 1 Corinthians 13:2; Ephesians 3:4-5; Romans 16: 25-27); (3) discerning the hand of God in the present and in the future. So prophets ranked just below apostles in the early church.

Agabus was one of these prophets. He foretold a famine that came in A.D. 46 in Palestine. The disciples believed the prophecy. So they took a collection to help those who would be hungry. And they sent the collection to the "brethren who lived in Judea" by Barnabas and Paul. (See Acts 11:27-30.)

Being sent to Jerusalem was a great event in the life of Paul. Paul's conversion was probably in A.D. 31. His first brief visit to Jerusalem with Barnabas was in AD. 33. The "famine visit" was in A.D. 46. He reported to the Jerusalem church that a fellowship of Greek Christians was thriving in Antioch. Paul and Barnabas gave the gift for "famine" relief. And they also explained to Peter, James, and the other apostles the fantastic response to Christ in pagan Antioch.

Paul had spent three years in Arabia immediately after his conversion. He had then spent ten more years in Cilicia and Syria. During these years he had found himself as a Christian. He had carefully thought through his beliefs about God and Christ. He had had many years of experience as a missionary to Jews and Gentiles. But when he left Antioch for Jerusalem, he was uneasy and excited about meeting the apostles and elders of the church in Jerusalem. And, of course, the leaders in Jerusalem appreciated the gift of money.

A NEW WAVE OF PERSECUTION
Acts 12:1-3

About that time Herod the king laid violent hands upon some who belonged to the church. He killed James the brother of John with the sword; and when he saw that it pleased the Jews, he proceeded to arrest Peter also.

Read all of Acts 12 in your Bibles for thorough understanding of this section. The first three words *about that time* suggest something about how Luke wrote his Gospel and Acts. He told about one event and the persons involved. Then he told about another event. But he did not always tell about events in the order they happened.

The last verse of Acts 11 tells about Barnabas and Paul taking the famine money to the brethren in Judea. The year is A.D. 46. But Acts 12 begins with an account of Herod the king, who ruled from A.D. 41 to 44. So Herod died two years before Paul and

Barnabas took the famine money to Judea. Luke covers this two-year time difference with the phrase *about that time*. Luke told about Paul and Barnabas (A.D. 46). Then he returned to his account of Peter (A.D. 44). To put it in our words: "A couple of years before Paul took the collection to Jerusalem, King Herod had laid violent hands upon the church. . . ." For example, he killed James, the son of Zebedee. According to tradition, he may also have killed James's brother John at this time. Why did he do so? Who was this Herod?

[Note that two Jameses are mentioned in Acts 12. Do not confuse James, the son of Zebedee (Acts 12:2), and James, the brother of Jesus (Acts 12:17).]

We are talking about Herod Agrippa I, who was crowned king of Judea in A.D. 41. He was the grandson of Herod the Great. Agrippa I lived in Rome most of his life. He was crowned king while still in Rome by his crony, the mad Emperor Caligula.

When he became king of Judea, Agrippa I returned to Jerusalem and sought to win favor with the Jews. He was a clever, ingenious politician. Like his forebears, he ruled by pretending to be interested in the law of the Jews. He wanted to prove his loyalty to the law. One way he found was to persecute the Nazarenes (Christians). The deaths of James and John were the fruit of his shrewd political mind.

Under this persecution Peter was arrested. He too was sentenced to death. Four squads of soldiers took turns guarding him. Four soldiers formed each squad. Two guarded the door. He was chained between the other two guards.

A TESTIMONY OF EARNEST PRAYER
Acts 12:5-17

So Peter was kept in prison; but earnest prayer for him was made to God by the church.

. . . and behold, an angel of the Lord appeared. . . . And the chains fell off his hands. . . . And Peter . . . said, "Now I am sure that the Lord has sent his angel and rescued me from the hand of Herod and from all that the Jewish people were expecting." (Acts 12:5, 7, 11)

Try to imagine what Peter did during a week in prison. Formerly, he had witnessed to Samaritans. He had been used by God to heal the lame. He had confirmed Philip's ministry in Lydda, Joppa, and Caesarea. Now in prison he could do only one thing. He witnessed to his jailers. (Luke does not say so. But isn't this just what Peter would have done?) Those soldiers chained to his wrists must have heard him sing, pray, and explain the Scriptures. His prayers must have included their names. Peter lifted his captors to the throne of

grace. What a contrast to his cowardly action in Luke 22:56-60, when he denied his Lord.

Add to Peter's witnessing spirit the earnest prayer of the Jerusalem church for him. His spirit and their prayers brought on a release from prison that would not otherwise have happened. Luke's word for "earnest prayer" is the same word he used to tell how Jesus prayed at Gethsemane. So the Christians at Mary's home prayed for Peter as Jesus prayed at Gethsemane.

Christians should have no doubt that often "earnest prayer" unlocks doors, even prison doors. We must not get lost in asking how miracles happen. We should get lost in the wonder of God's liberating action.

We should admit openly that God does not always rescue us from our prisons. God did not save Stephen's life, nor James's. Yet he did give them power to live through their persecutions victoriously. God may not rescue you from evil, but he is with you through it all. Emmanuel! God is with us! We are sons of the covenant.

When Peter left the prison, he went directly to Mary's home. He must have gone with some uncertainty, because of the persecution of the church. When he got to her house, James and "the brethren" were not there. (Acts 12:17) They may have been in hiding.

Knocking on the door, Peter called to a slave girl, Rhoda. She was so overjoyed that she completely forgot his need. In her enthusiasm for what God had done she forgot what Peter needed most—to have her open the door. Instead, she ran to tell others the good news.

Peter told them to tell James and the brethren what had happened. "Then he departed and went to another place." (Acts 12:17) Luke did not reveal the secret hiding place they had gone to in those days.

> Now when day came, there was no small stir among the soldiers over what had become of Peter. And when Herod had sought for him and could not find him, he examined the sentries and ordered that they should be put to death. Then he went down from Judea to Caesarea, and remained there.
>
> ... On an appointed day Herod put on his royal robes, took his seat upon the throne, and made an oration to them. And the people shouted, "The voice of a god, and not of man!" Immediately an angel of the Lord smote him, because he did not give God the glory; and he was eaten by worms and died. (Acts 12:18-23)

Josephus, an ancient historian of the Jews, states that there was a festival for Herod. On the second day of the festival, Herod entered the theater clad in a robe of silver. The sun glinted on the silver. The people had to shade their eyes to look in his direction, and they cried out that this was a god come to them.

This lesson mentions Cyprus, Antioch of Syria, Tarsus, and Jerusalem. This map shows their location. The site of Antioch of Syria, now called Antakya, is in modern Turkey.

From *The Interpreter's Dictionary of the Bible* Copyright © 1962 by Abingdon Press

"An angel of the Lord smote him . . . and he was eaten by worms and died." What a remarkable sentence. The Greek word for "eaten by worms" is *skolekobrotos*. This word is an agricultural term that refers to diseased grain. King Herod Agrippa I was like grain with the kernel eaten away. Only the shell is left. The nutritive value was eaten up. He was an empty man. He was a shell of a man. Pompous, he had the outer splendor of a god but was empty within. He knew little of spiritual values. He knew little of love, patience, or hope. He had no deep yearning to know and to do the will of God. He sought only pleasure, pride, power, and prestige. "An angel of the Lord smote him." God always punishes such emptiness. According to Luke, the king died because he persecuted the church.

When Herod persecuted the church and killed its leaders, who was really killed? James? John? Or Herod? To some persons, death has no sting. The lives of others are so shallow and empty that God will not honor them with eternal life.

Every man has this choice. He can choose an abundant life or an empty death. Some pagans (like those at Antioch) respond positively to Christ. Some pagans (like Herod Agrippa I) reject and attempt to destroy Christ. And in the process they destroy themselves.

Saint Paul, by El Greco
The St. Louis Art Museum

This portrait of Paul shows him with a sword. Legends say that Paul was beheaded. The sword represents his death as a martyr.

8. Set Apart for Mission
(Acts 12:25 through 14:20)

Luke loved the Lord and the church's mission. He loved those who carried its message to the ends of the world. We are grateful that he wrote an orderly account of how the good news spread from Jerusalem to Rome.

So far we have studied three major sections of Acts: (1) Acts 1:1 through 6:7, the church in Jerusalem and the preaching of Peter; (2) Acts 6:8 through 9:31, the expansion of the church through Palestine; (3) Acts 9:32 through 12:24, the expansion of the church to Antioch.

Now we are ready to study Luke's fourth section, Acts 12:25 through 16:5. This section tells of the church moving into Asia Minor, with emphasis on Galatia. (See map on page 66.)

Read all of Acts 12:25 through 14:28 before you begin to study this lesson.

In Acts 12 Luke goes back to the story of Paul and Barnabas. During the famine they had taken a gift from Antioch to Jerusalem. Luke says that Barnabas and Saul returned from Jerusalem when they had fulfilled their mission, bringing with them John whose other name was Mark. (See Acts 12:25.) Now the scene shifts back to Antioch.

FOREIGN MISSION IS BORN
Acts 13:1-3

The church in Antioch did a pioneering thing. They sent men to other countries to try to win Gentiles to the faith.

> **Now in the church at Antioch there were prophets and teachers, Barnabas, Simeon who was called Niger, Lucius of Cyrene, Manaen a member of the court of Herod the tetrarch, and Saul. While they were worshiping the Lord and fasting, the Holy Spirit said, "Set apart for me Barnabas and Saul for the work to which I have called them." (Acts 13:1-2)**

Who were these prophets and teachers of Antioch who sent out the first Christian missionaries? Five men are listed in Acts.

61

(1) *Barnabas* we have met previously. He was from Cyprus. He was a kind, encouraging, and generous man. He was deeply committed to Christ and to spreading the good news to Cyprus, his home, and to Asia Minor.

(2) *Simeon Niger* was from North Africa.

(3) *Lucius* was a teacher and prophet of Cyrene. He may have been the kinsman of Paul mentioned in Roman 16:21. If so, he became a companion of Paul in Europe.

(4) *Manaen* was "a member of the court of Herod the tetrarch." He was apparently educated with Herod Antipas, who governed Galilee in the days of Jesus. (Luke 3:1; 9:7) As a member of Herod's staff, Manaen had considerable authority.

(5) *Saul* is Paul, whose conversion made him the apostle to the Gentiles. He was called by the risen Christ to this rank and responsibility. In a sense he replaced Judas Iscariot as the twelfth apostle. The method of drawing lots (as Matthias was chosen in Acts 1:26) was not Christ's method. Christ *called* Paul to be his apostle.

What a group of prophets and teachers these five were. Each of them was concerned about God's love for Gentiles. Each prayed about God's will for Gentiles. Each obeyed the dictates of the Holy Spirit. As "they were worshiping the Lord and fasting, the Holy Spirit said, 'Set apart for me Barnabas and Saul. . . .' Then after fasting and praying they [the churchmen at Antioch] laid their hands on them and sent them off." (Acts 13:2-3) The laying on of hands blessed Paul and Barnabas as they became missionaries. Paul and Barnabas did not go out alone. The Christians at Antioch sent a young man from Jerusalem with them. "And they had John to assist them." (Acts 13:5)

THE CLASH OF MAGIC AND RELIGION
Acts 13:4-12

When they had gone through the whole island as far as Paphos, they came upon a certain magician, a Jewish false prophet, named Bar-Jesus. . . . But Saul, who is also called Paul, filled with the Holy Spirit, looked intently at him and said, "You son of the devil, you enemy of all righteousness, full of all deceit and villainy, will you not stop making crooked the straight paths of the Lord?" (Acts 13:6, 9-10)

Paul, Barnabas, and John Mark went to the island of Cyprus. (See the map on page 59.) They went to Paphos, the capital of Cyprus. Paphos was famous for its temple to Aphrodite. The worshipers of Aphrodite encouraged lustful immorality in the name of their religion. Paphos was also noted for a magician (similar to Simon Magus, Acts 8:9). This magician was Elymas, a sorcerer and false prophet. He was a personal employee of the ruler, who was Sergius Paulus, a man of intelligence. (Acts 13:7) Sergius Paulus summoned Barnabas and Paul in order to hear the word of God. A clash between the man of magic, Elymas, and the man of faith, Paul, was inevitable.

Elymas, known also as Bar-Jesus, "withstood them, seeking to turn away the proconsul from the faith." (Acts 13:8) Elymas was not interested in faith. He was interested in magic. The difference is significant. Magic seeks to bend the will of God to the will of man. Man through magic tries to control God's laws through the power of secret knowledge. This power he might use for the benefit of his clients who could pay for his services. Magic uses God and his laws selfishly. Magic does not seek to worship or to serve him. False prophets, such as Elymas, were interested in religion. But their interest was not Godward. Rather, Elymas tried to use religion for his own private purposes. His religion was a means to an end. He had no interest in spiritual values as such.

False prophets appear in every age. In the 1970's we find persons who come close to the spirit of Elymas. They suggest that men should become Christians because being known as a Christian is good for business, brings peace of mind, overcomes insomnia, or drives out illness. But these reasons are not of first importance. The primary goal of religion is to lead a man to God and nurture his life of faith.

Against this background we understand Paul's angry statement to Elymas: "You son of the devil . . . will you not stop making crooked the straight paths of the Lord?" (Acts 13:10)

Paul spoke harshly to Elymas, but Paul may have said just exactly what Elymas needed to hear: You are a quack. A fake. Paul simply told him what he was—a charlatan! He was an obstacle to faith. He was a hindrance to understanding. He was blind to the Son of God.

And Sergius Paulus, the proconsul, heard Paul's message with favor. He may even have been converted. (Acts 13:12)

THE GALATIAN CHURCHES
Acts 13:13 through 14:20

> Now Paul and his company set sail from Paphos, and came to Perga in Pamphylia. And John left them and returned to Jerusalem; but they passed on from Perga and came to Antioch of Pisidia. And on the sabbath day they went into the synagogue and sat down. (Acts 13:13-14)

The phrase *Now Paul and his company* is important. For Luke, Paul's leadership began at this moment in history. Previously Luke used the phrase *Barnabas and Saul*. Now Paul is the leader. Even his name has changed from the Jewish *Saul* to the Latin *Paulus* (Paul, in English). Perhaps he assumed his Latin name because he planned now to address himself to Gentiles.

Paul's company included Barnabas and John Mark. For some unknown reason John Mark left Paul. Possibly John Mark was jealous. Paul became the leader and John's beloved cousin, Barnabas, took second place. Of course, John Mark simply may have wanted to go home to Jerusalem.

Paul and Barnabas had begun this journey in Antioch of Syria. They now came to a second Antioch. What kind of city was this Antioch of Pisidia? (1) The city was 3600 feet above sea level. It was a center of Greek influence. It lay on the trade route between Ephesus and Cilicia. (2) Antioch was a free city. This means that its citizens were all Roman citizens. (3) Antioch had been colonized by Jews, under order of the Seleucid kings. The Jews had been transplanted here for business, cultural, and political reasons. They were good businessmen and cultured to a certain extent. They were literate. Many of them spoke more than one language. Because of these friendly Jews Paul could get a hearing in Antioch. Their synagogues were open to him.

Paul states that he preached in Antioch because he was sick. "You know it was because of a bodily ailment that I preached the gospel to you at first; and though my condition was a trial to you, you did not scorn or despise me, but received me as an angel of God, as Christ Jesus." (Galatians 4:13-14) Possibly Paul caught malaria while he was on the coast of Perga. If so, he may have gone to Antioch for its high altitude. Such a sickness (his "thorn . . . in the flesh," 2 Corinthians 12:7) led him to preach in the cities of Galatia—Antioch of Pisidia, Derbe, Lystra, and Iconium.

> **After the reading of the law and the prophets, the rulers of the synagogue sent to them, saying, "Brethren, if you have any word of exhortation for the people, say it." So Paul stood up, and motioning with his hand said:**
>
> **"Men of Israel, and you that fear God, listen." (Acts 13:15-16)**

In Antioch Paul and Barnabas went to the synagogue first. The order of service, the same throughout the world, included: (1) reciting Deuteronomy 6:4-9 (the *Shema*) in unison, (2) praying by the leader or ruler of the synagogue, (3) reading a section of the law, (4) reading a section of the prophets, (5) an address, and (6) the benediction (Numbers 6:24-26). The rulers of the synagogue asked Paul, as a learned rabbi and traveler, to interpret the Scriptures. Paul did. This was the address, listed above as the fifth part of the service.

Paul's address (Acts 13:16-47) is a typical Christian sermon to the Jews, whom he seeks to convert. A modern Christian needs to know how the early church used its Old Testament. Paul's sermon is a good example of that use.

Here are the basic biblical points in Paul's sermon.

(1) God fulfilled his threefold covenant with Abraham. (See Genesis 12:1-7.) (a) God made the people Israel a great nation. (b) He gave them the land of Canaan for an inheritance. (c) Through Jesus, a descendant of Abraham, he blessed all mankind. In this statement Paul also affirmed the ancient creed of Israel. (See Deuteronomy 26:5-9.) He appealed to the sons of the covenant. He said that God keeps his promises.

(2) The son of David (the "stock of Jesse") had come as God promised. "Of this man's [King David's] posterity God has brought to Israel a *Savior,* Jesus, as he promised. . . . to us has been sent the message of this salvation." (Acts 13:23, 26*b*, italics added.) The Jews had waited long for the Davidic promise to be fulfilled. In Jesus' day the people looked for a person appointed by God who would start a new age for God's people. That Messiah had come. Jesus was that Messiah. He brought a new era.

(3) Jesus' crucifixion was part of God's plan. Furthermore, "God raised him from the dead." (Acts 13:30) The Resurrection was the proof that Jesus was the Christ (Messiah).

(4) "And we bring you *the good news* that what God promised to the fathers, this he has fulfilled to us their children by raising Jesus." (Acts 13:32-33) Paul was helping the Jews and God-fearers see that God's action was contemporary. His covenant was being renewed. New things were happening by the hands of God.

(5) By this action came forgiveness of sins, a new beginning, a new life.

The only requirement God made of Abraham was that he trust God. Trust alone undergirds the covenant. When persons trust one another, their covenant is firm. Family members who trust one another are not obsessed by rules. Rules will take care of themselves. Where trust is, a member of the family can break an accepted rule, yet receive a second chance. Paul calls the sinners back into trust and confidence. He calls them to accept a new covenant founded on Jesus Christ.

The Jews and converts of Judaism urged Paul to speak the next sabbath. But he did not, for jealousy created friction. Within a week

Paul and Barnabas told the Jews of Antioch that they would leave them and take their message to the Gentiles. This fulfilled the prophecy of Isaiah. He said the Jews would "be a light for the Gentiles" and would "bring salvation to the uttermost parts of the earth." (Acts 13:47. See also Isaiah 49:6.) The Gentiles approved, but the Jews objected. Soon Paul and Barnabas were on their way to another city.

Now at Iconium they entered together into the Jewish synagogue. . . . But the people of the city were divided. . . . (Acts 14:1, 4)

Though many were converted, little was achieved in Iconium. The city was divided, suspicious, antagonistic. Here at Iconium Paul and Barnabas were called "apostles" for the first time.

From *The Interpreter's Dictionary of the Bible*
Copyright © 1962 by Abingdon Press

This lesson mentions Pamphylia, Antioch of Pisidia, Iconium, Lystra, and Derbe. This map shows their location. The area shown in this map is in modern Turkey.

> Now at Lystra there was a man sitting, who could not use his feet; he was a cripple from birth, who had never walked. He listened to Paul speaking; and Paul . . . said in a loud voice, "Stand upright on your feet." And he sprang up and walked. . . . they [crowds] lifted up their voices, saying in Lycaonian, "The gods have come down to us in the likeness of men!" (Acts 14:8-11)

Read Acts 14:8-20. The natives of Lystra knew an ancient legend by heart. The legend says that the Greek gods Zeus and Hermes once came to earth in disguise. No one on earth offered them hospitality, except a peasant man and his wife, Philemon and Baucis. Everybody else threw stones at them. The townspeople turned their dogs on the gods. As a result, the gods blessed the two peasants, but destroyed the countryside, people, crops, and animals. So when Paul healed a cripple, the people were so excited they cried, "The gods have come down to us in the likeness of men!" The crowd remembered the legend. They did not want to make the same mistake again. So they acclaimed the two apostles as gods.

From Paul's response we learn how he approached persons who were completely heathen. He made two points. (1) He preached God as the Creator. (Acts 14:15) He did not preach Christ at this time. He started with an understanding the people already had. (2) He preached that God "did not leave himself without witness." (Acts 14:17) He made a similar point in Romans 1:19-20 and again in his address in Athens. (See Acts 17:19-31.) We shall study the latter in detail later.

Obviously Paul planned to follow these two points with his message that God had appointed Jesus Christ as Savior. But he did not get that far. Some Jews from Antioch and Iconium were in Lystra. They led a riot. They stoned Paul and dragged his body, which they thought was dead, outside the city walls. "But when the disciples gathered about him, he rose up and entered the city." (Acts 14:20) Imagine. Paul was stoned and left for dead. Yet he turned right around and entered the city to preach again. What courage and persistence in mission!

9. God Opens a Door of Faith
(Acts 14:21 through 16:5)

Luke portrays Paul as an invincible crusader. He could preach, teach, and heal. At Lystra he was stoned. Yet in love he returned to Lystra and to those who ordered him out of their city. (See Acts 14:19-21.)

This lesson ends the fourth section of Acts. This section is an account of how the church moved into Asia Minor. In this section Luke tells more about Paul's mission to the cities of southern Galatia. Barnabas was still with Paul. We have read of their Galatian ministry in Antioch, Iconium, and Lystra. They stayed a brief and fruitful time in Derbe. Then they returned to these same cities on their way back to Antioch of Syria. Then they went on to Jerusalem.

Read Acts 14:21 through 16:5.

GOD OPENS A DOOR OF FAITH
Acts 14:21-28

. . . they returned to Lystra and to Iconium and to Antioch, strengthening the souls of the disciples, exhorting them to continue in the faith, and saying that through many tribulations we must enter the kingdom of God. . . . they sailed to Antioch. . . . And when they arrived, they . . . declared . . . how he [God] had opened a door of faith to the Gentiles. (Acts 14:21-22, 26-27)

Paul and Barnabas did three things as they visited again the churches they had founded. (1) They strengthened the new disciples. They helped them understand how to use their (Jewish) Bible. They taught them how to pray and how to seek guidance from the Holy

This portrait of Paul shows him as a fierce crusader.

68

Saint Paul, by Vincenzo Foppa
New Orleans Museum of Art, Samuel H. Kress Collection

Spirit. (2) They urged them to continue in the faith. They taught
that suffering is the way into the kingdom of God. Christ suffered.
He still suffers. His followers must suffer. But through such suffering
men may enter the kingdom of God. (3) Paul and Barnabas talked
about leadership for each new congregation. Then the new Christians
voted to decide who their elders would be. Our text says "they
had *appointed* elders. . . ." The Greek verb means "to take a vote."
So the elders were "appointed" by democratic process. Upon their
return to Antioch in Syria, Paul and Barnabas praised God for what
he had done. They told "how he had opened a door of faith to the
Gentiles." A remarkable fact is that no one grumbled about a rough
trip. We read no sour words about how poorly they were treated,
even though they had faced many kinds of bitterness. Paul had even
been stoned. Instead, they thanked God because he had opened the
door of faith to the Gentiles.

Consider the phrase *opened a door*. An open door makes us think
of fresh air, new life, and new horizons. God opened a door to
the Gentiles. They needed only to walk through the door into a new
day, a new age, a new world. From beginning to end, Paul's journey
to the Gentiles had been directed by God. Paul's mission was begun,
directed, and made powerful by God.

But how would the Jewish Christians in Jerusalem react to a
mission to Gentiles? Some of Paul's converts did not attend synagogue
worship. Some did not follow the food laws of the Jews. They were
not circumcised. But they *did* understand God and the Messiah he
had sent for their redemption. They more than understood. They
embraced the good news until it was their own. These Gentile people
became a part of God's new covenant.

Could the church in Jerusalem accept these new converts? Needless
to say, Gentile Christianity was a hot religious issue in Jerusalem.
Could the church include converts who did not obey the laws of
Moses?

DISSENSION ARISES
Acts 15:1-2

> But some men came down from Judea and were teaching the
> brethren, "Unless you are circumcised according to the custom of
> Moses, you cannot be saved." And when Paul and Barnabas had
> no small dissension and debate with them, Paul and Barnabas and
> some of the others were appointed to go up to Jerusalem to the
> apostles and the elders about this question.

Some Christian Jews from Jerusalem came to Antioch. They were
loyal both to the risen Christ and to the law of Moses. They believed

that Gentile Christians must be circumcised. That is, they must live according to the law of Moses. These Christians from Jerusalem argued that only so can a person be saved.

We must understand these loyal churchmen who were deeply rooted in Judaism. They were probably Pharisees, as James, the brother of Jesus, had been at one time. The word *Pharisee* means "separated." Pharisees were separated from other Jews by their intense obedience to the written law and to the oral law. Many Christians who had once been Pharisees remained loyal to the law after their conversion to Christ.

The written law was the first five books of our Bible, called the Pentateuch. This law included rules about festivals, the sabbath, rituals, ceremonial cleanliness, and so forth. The oral or unwritten law added thousands of interpretations and applications to the written law. For example, oral law forbade walking in the fields on the sabbath. Why? While walking, a person might break a blade of grass, in which case he would be mowing grass on the sabbath. Or, a Pharisee dared not walk in the woods on the sabbath, for fear he might break a twig. Why? Breaking a twig was equal to chopping wood on the sabbath. There were hundreds of other unwritten rules about breaking the sabbath.

The Pharisee was sincere about all this. The Pharisees would not take up arms on the sabbath. To carry arms on the sabbath was work. In a revolution that took place in 168 B.C., they chose to die rather than to defend themselves on the sabbath.

We see this deep-seated loyalty to the law in the concern of the Christian Jews who came to Antioch. They saw the foundations of Judaism at stake.

The Pharisees were not unprogressive people. They were the very Jews who first included the prophets, Jonah, Ruth, and Psalms in the Bible. They accepted new forms of worship. They adopted the new festivals of Hanukkah and Purim. They baptized converts. They believed in the resurrection of the body in the life to come. The Pharisees embodied Psalms 119:97: "Oh, how I love thy law! It is my meditation all the day."

From this group of dedicated Pharisees came some converts to Christ. Their concern to obey the law was no light matter. So they demanded that all Christians also obey the law. In Antioch they tried to force this demand on *Gentile* Christians. "And when Paul and Barnabas had no small dissension and debate with them, Paul and Barnabas and some of the others were appointed to go up to Jerusalem to the apostles and the elders about this question." (Acts 15:2)

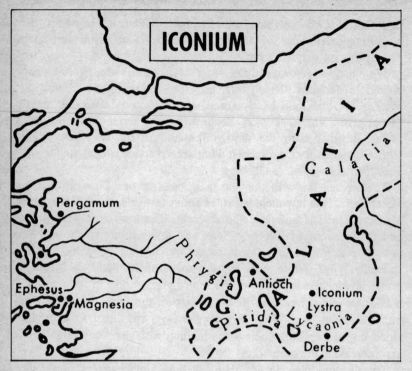

From *The Interpreter's Dictionary of the Bible*
Copyright © 1962 by Abingdon Press

This lesson mentions Galatia. The map shows that Galatia contained Antioch of Pisidia, Iconium, Lystra, and Derbe.

The questions were these. Must *Gentile* converts be circumcised? Must they obey the laws of the Pentateuch? Must they obey the Jewish laws about clean and unclean foods?

THE EARLY CHURCH DEBATES
Acts 15:3-35

When they came to Jerusalem, they were welcomed by the church and the apostles and the elders, and they declared all that God had done with them. But some believers who belonged to the party of the Pharisees rose up, and said, "It is necessary to circum-

║ cise them, and to charge them to keep the law of Moses." (Acts ║ 15:4-5)

As Paul and Barnabas walked toward Jerusalem, they visited the churches of Phoenicia and Samaria. Everywhere they went, their faith created expressions of happiness and joy. What a fine background for their entrance into Jerusalem and their appearance before the elders!

James, the brother of Jesus, was at this time the head of the church in Jerusalem.

Let us note several things about this James. (1) He was the head of the church in Jerusalem. (2) He had been a Pharisee, as had Paul. We may imagine that Jesus and James had strong differences of opinion in their youth. (3) At first, James did not accept his brother as the Messiah. (John 7:5) (4) James the Pharisee thought his brother Jesus had lost his reason. He thought Jesus was mad. (Mark 3:21) (5) James had possibly seen and certainly heard about his brother's death. (6) Jesus made a special Resurrection appearance to James. (1 Corinthians 15:7) Perhaps the Lord told him to assume leadership of his followers in Jerusalem. (7) He died as a martyr in A.D. 61.

In Jerusalem the apostles and elders welcomed them. Paul and Barnabas told about God's work among the Gentiles. They told of signs and wonders in Antioch, Lystra, and Iconium. They concluded that God does not limit his new covenant to one race or one nation or one religion. In Asia Minor God had filled Gentile converts with his Spirit. They had been baptized. *But none had been circumcised.*

Some Pharisee Christians arose immediately and spoke like this: That, Paul, is precisely the point. You and Barnabas should have required these Gentile converts to become Jews after their conversion. They are not yet circumcised as required by the law. So they are not yet acceptable members of the church.

║ The apostles and the elders were gathered together to consider ║ this matter. (Acts 15:6)

So a long debate began. The apostles and elders listened to two sides. (1) The Pharisee Christians spoke of their concern for the law. (2) Then the prophets and teachers from Antioch spoke of the Spirit's harvest among Gentiles. Much debate followed. (Acts 15:7) After the debate, four persons summarized their opinions: Peter, Paul, Barnabas, and James. This council showed an openness to differing religious opinions. Christians of various views were present and spoke. Let us consider the various attitudes separately.

Read Galatians 2 as further background for Acts 15.

Let us assume that Paul wrote his Letter to the Galatians in A.D.

48, just before he came to this council meeting in Jerusalem in A.D. 49. If so, this meeting may have embarrassed Peter. For he had to face Paul, who had scolded him for refusing to eat with the Gentile Christians at Antioch. In Paul's Letter to the Galatians (2:11-16) he tells that he had to oppose Peter (Cephas) in Antioch:

But when Cephas came to Antioch I opposed him to his face, because he stood condemned. For before certain men came from James, he ate with the Gentiles; but when they came he drew back and separated himself, fearing the circumcision party. And with him the rest of the Jews acted insincerely, so that even Barnabas was carried away by their insincerity. (Galatians 2:11-13)

This quarrel between Paul and Peter happened before the conference in Jerusalem described in Acts 15.

The quarrel described in Galatians 2 was over social relationships in the church. Could Christian Jews eat with Christian Gentiles? Could Jews, even Christian Jews, eat with men who did not observe Jewish customs about clean and unclean foods?

Peter had eaten at the home of Cornelius. He even slept there. He did a similar thing in Antioch when he visited the churches there. But some Pharisee Christians came from Jerusalem and pointed out that Peter was acting unlawfully. He was eating unclean foods and sitting at the same table with uncircumcised Gentiles. Peter weakly left the Gentiles and sat with the Christian Jews.

Paul was furious. He told Peter, "If you, though a Jew, live like a Gentile and not like a Jew, how can you compel the Gentiles to live like Jews?" (Galatians 2:14) A man is not justified by works of the law, Paul said, but by grace through faith in Jesus Christ.

Now let's go back to Acts 15 and the Council. Peter said that he supported Paul's position about the Gentiles. He reminded the apostles that God revealed to him in a vision that Gentiles are clean. All things made by God are good. (See Acts 10.) Peter said in effect: Though the Gentiles do not keep the Jewish laws of purity, God has nonetheless cleansed their hearts by faith. (Acts 15:9) God looks on the inner man, not the outer man. God alone decides who shall belong to the covenant community. Men do not find salvation by obeying rules. They are saved by commitment to Christ and by faith in his life and purposes.

Peter's statement was in line with the Sermon on the Mount. Jesus kept the Ten Commandments, but he did more. He was careful about attitudes that might lead to murder, adultery, or theft. In morality the attitude comes before the act. A religion of rules is a religion that relies on human merit. But man is not saved by obeying rules. He is saved by grace through faith. He is saved by his attitude toward Christ, toward the purposes of God, toward man, and toward the world.

> **And all the assembly kept silence; and they listened to Barnabas and Paul as they related what signs and wonders God had done through them among the Gentiles. (Acts 15:12)**

Paul must have nodded at Peter. Peter remembered well how the cock crowed three times. He remembered how he timidly refused to eat with Gentiles.

Paul and Barnabas simply told what God was doing among the Gentiles. The Gentiles had responded to the gospel message. They had been filled with the Holy Spirit. They loved Christ and molded their ways after his. When Paul sat down, another period of silence must have followed.

> **After they finished speaking, James replied, "Brethren, listen to me. Simeon [Simon Peter] has related how God first visited the Gentiles, to take out of them a people for his name. And with this the words of the prophets agree, as it is written. . . . Therefore my judgment is that we should not trouble those of the Gentiles who turn to God, but should write to them to abstain from the pollutions of idols and from unchastity and from what is strangled and from blood. . . ." (Acts 15:13-15, 19-20)**

James was a Pharisee before he became a Christian. Now he spoke as head of the church. He quoted the prophet Amos to support his belief that Gentiles are included in God's plan. Through Jesus God is rebuilding the house of David. Now all persons may seek the Lord. James agreed that Gentiles need not be circumcised. That is, they need not obey the law of Moses. This supported Paul and Barnabas.

James decreed that a letter be written. It should state the policy of the church toward Gentiles. For Gentile converts there were to be three requirements. These requirements yielded three points to the Pharisee-Christian view. The Gentile Christians were to realize that the church included Jews. So for the sake of fellowship they should follow three rules. (1) They should not eat anything that had been strangled, since eating the blood was contrary to the law. The blood holds the life of the animal, and the life belongs to God. But the meat belongs to and can be eaten by men. (2) They should not eat meat offered to idols since it had been dedicated to the god to whom it was offered. (3) Chastity should be observed.

We should note that the Council reached this decision on the basis that it was *scriptural* (James quoted Amos) and upheld by the *experiences* of Peter, Barnabas, and Paul. And it was a *reasonable* conclusion.

The apostles and elders agreed with James. They wrote a letter that contained James's suggestions. Then they chose Judas and Silas, "leading men among the brethren," to take the letter to Antioch. So Judas and Silas, accompanied by Paul and Barnabas, went to the church of Antioch to report the decision of the Apostolic Council. After making their personal report, supported by the letter, Judas and Silas returned to Jerusalem. Later Silas agreed to go with Paul on another tour.

PAUL PREPARES FOR HIS EUROPEAN MISSION
Acts 15:36 through 16:5

And after some days Paul said to Barnabas, "Come, let us return and visit the brethren in every city where we proclaimed the word of the Lord, and see how they are." (Acts 15:36)

Paul and Barnabas separated. Barnabas wanted John Mark to go with them. But Paul balked. John Mark had failed once. Why try him a second time? Barnabas demanded a second chance for John Mark. Paul won. So Barnabas took John Mark with him to Cyprus. And Paul took Silas. Paul and Silas went through Galatia, visiting again in Lystra, Iconium, and Antioch. At Lystra Paul asked Timothy to come with him.

Timothy's mother and grandmother were Christians. He became Paul's "beloved son." Timothy, half Greek and half Jew, was circumcised so he would be free to work with Jews as well as Gentiles. These two became lifelong companions. Timothy was with Paul in Thessalonica, Beroea, Corinth, Philippi, and Ephesus. He wrote several of Paul's letters as his secretary.

So the way was paved for the mission to Europe.

10. Guided by God
(Acts 16:6 through 17:34)

Luke wanted Theophilus and all others who love God to have an account of the spread of Christianity throughout the world. To do this, Luke wrote The Acts of the Apostles in six sections. We have studied four of these: (1) Acts 1:1 through 6:7, the church begins in Jerusalem; (2) Acts 6:8 through 9:31, the church spreads through Palestine (Samaria, Lydda, Joppa, Caesarea); (3) Acts 9:32 through 12:24, the church reaches Antioch; (4) Acts 12:25 through 16:5, the church is planted in Asia Minor and Galatia.

Now we begin the fifth section of Luke's book, Acts 16:6 through 19:20. The next two lessons are based on this fifth section of Acts. Read Acts 16:6 through 17:34.

Paul and Silas visited again the Galatian churches that Paul and Barnabas had founded. But he and Silas were not certain where to go next. (Acts 15:36 through 16:5) Paul made two attempts to continue his mission. Each time he was told by the Holy Spirit that he should not take the route he had chosen. Here and throughout Acts the Holy Spirit directs the growth of the church. (Acts 16:6-8)

SOME MISSION AREAS WERE "OFF LIMITS"
Acts 16:6-10

> **And they went through the region of Phrygia and Galatia, having been forbidden by the Holy Spirit to speak the word in Asia. And when they had come opposite Mysia, they attempted to go into Bithynia, but the Spirit of Jesus did not allow them. . . . (Acts 16:6-7)**

Paul was a man guided by God. Yet, strangely, his mission to Europe came by way of disappointments. Twice the Spirit told him not to preach at specific places. (1) Paul and Silas went to the coastal areas around Ephesus. (Luke calls these areas "Asia." See the map on page 102.) But they were told by the Holy Spirit not to preach there. (2) They attempted to go northeast into Bithynia. Again the

Paintings of Luke often show an ox with wings. The ox with wings is the traditional symbol for Luke the evangelist.

St. Luke the Evangelist, by Giovanni di Paolo
National Gallery of Art

Spirit of Jesus did not allow them. Peter may have been working in Bithynia. That may be a reason Paul's work needed to be carried elsewhere. (See 1 Peter 1:1.)

Think about this. The places Paul wanted to go (Asia and Bithynia) were closed to him. In a sense God turned down Paul's first two choices. Finally a third choice came. And it became the greatest thing that could have happened to him. Certainly we can see an insight here for us when we are unable to do what we yearn to do most. Our third or fourth choice may be best for us.

Paul and Silas went west to the coast to Troas. Troas was on the extreme western edge of the Asian continent. While there, Paul learned through a vision where to preach next. The Spirit led Paul to a ministry in Greece. The gospel headed for Europe.

And a vision appeared to Paul in the night: a man of Macedonia was standing beseeching him and saying, "Come over to Macedonia and help us." And when he had seen the vision, immediately we

| sought to go on into Macedonia, concluding that God had called
| us to preach the gospel to them. (Acts 16:9-10)

What did Paul see in the vision? He saw a man of Macedonia. The word *Macedonia* refers to the area that is today the northern portion of modern Greece.

How did Paul happen to be thinking of Macedonia? Is it possible that his vision was influenced by Alexander the Great? Alexander the Great was the greatest "man of Macedonia." He dreamed of one world, one language, and one culture. Perhaps that dream influenced Paul. He knew that Alexander's hope had gone unfulfilled. Paul might have reasoned that Alexander's dream of unity for mankind could be fulfilled only as men became one in Christ. Alexander's hope to marry the east to the west was a great hope. Even today Christians express this hope, because they know it can be real through commitment to Jesus Christ. Culture, technology, language, and armies cannot unite mankind. But faith can and will.

A vision from God guided Paul's footsteps to Macedonia (northern Greece) and Achaia (southern Greece). At this point, Luke enters the story. Possibly Paul had been sick and called at Luke's office for healing. They became good friends, fellow Christians, and companions. Beginning with Acts 16:10, Luke uses the pronoun *we*. After this point, Luke writes from firsthand experience, because he is traveling with Paul.

A RICH WOMAN AND A JAILER CONVERTED
Acts 16:11-40

| Setting sail therefore from Troas . . . to Philippi, which is the
| leading city of the district of Macedonia, and a Roman colony.
| . . . and on the sabbath day we went outside the gate to the
| riverside, where we supposed there was a place of prayer. . . .
| (Acts 16:11-13)

The father of Alexander the Great was Philip II of Macedonia. The city of Philippi was named in his honor. It was a Roman colony, whose citizens were Roman citizens. They governed themselves.

Paul and Silas, as was customary, first sought a synagogue. They found instead a place of prayer near the riverside. They sat down, as was the custom of those who were to preach, and spoke to the women who had come together. One of the converts was a rich woman, a seller of purple goods, an emigrant from the city of Thyatira. This woman, Lydia, was baptized, with her household. She was Paul's first European convert. Paul and Silas stayed at her house while they were in Philippi. (See Acts 16:13-15.)

During this first mission in Philippi, Paul was annoyed by "a slave girl who had a spirit of divination and brought her owners much gain by soothsaying." (Acts 16:16) Paul freed her from the evil spirit. Her owners were angered. Their source of income was gone. Soon Paul and Silas were arrested and put in jail.

> **But about midnight Paul and Silas were praying and singing hymns to God, and the prisoners were listening to them, and suddenly there was a great earthquake, so that the foundations of the prison were shaken; and immediately all the doors were opened and every one's fetters were unfastened. (Acts 16:25-26)**

That Paul and Silas could sing and pray in an underground prison is remarkable. But the significant event in this story is the answer they gave to the jailer's fearful question, "Men, what must I do to be saved?" (Acts 16:30)

We note from Paul's sermon five facets of salvation. (Acts 16: 30-34) (1) Believe in the Lord Jesus. To believe includes: (a) *accepting* God's purposes as we see them in the life of Jesus, and (b) *surrendering* to the love of God as it appears in Jesus. As we surrender, we receive a strong desire to do His will in all of life. (2) Listen to the word of the Lord. New converts need to know what God says about man, about the church, about himself, and about the risen Christ. (3) Care for the needy. Paul and Silas had been beaten. The jailer washed their wounds. Then he set food before them. To care for others, especially our former enemies, is a mark of salvation. (4) Become members of the church. Faith grows in fellowship. (5) Rejoice.

Before Paul left Philippi, he demanded that the city officials apologize. They had beaten Roman citizens, Paul and Silas. (Acts 16:37) It was against the Roman law for anyone to flog a Roman citizen. The city officials were afraid. They came to Paul and Silas, apologized, and asked them to leave the city. (Acts 16:38-39) The officials were afraid for their jobs. They could be removed from office for being so careless. Paul and Silas, with aching backs, accepted their apologies. And they took their time about leaving the city. First they visited Lydia. They saw the brethren and spoke to them. Their words gave the young church fresh courage. (Acts 16:40) Imagine how their words strengthened the Philippian church. Paul and Silas had suffered for the Philippians. Suffering love converts and comforts others. Paul and Silas comforted their converts. Then they left Philippi.

MEN WHO TURNED THE WORLD UPSIDE DOWN
Acts 17:1-15

> **"These men who have turned the world upside down have come**

here also, and Jason has received them; and they are all acting against the decrees of Caesar, saying that there is another king, Jesus." (Acts 17:6-7)

Paul and Silas went next to Thessalonica and Beroea. In each city they caused an uproar. Paul told the Jews that the Messiah had come. The Messiah was Jesus of Nazareth. The Jews may have said, "So far, so good." The anger of the Jews arose at the next claim. "It was necessary for the Christ to suffer and to rise from the dead." No Jew could easily accept the idea of a suffering Messiah. How could the Messiah be sovereign if he suffered? A man who died on a cross was cursed. He could not be the anointed one. The anointed Messiah would be a victor, not a victim.

To the anger of the Jews was added the hostility of the Greeks. The Greeks believed that spirit and matter cannot mix. Matter is evil. Spirit is good. Death separates the spirit from the body. Death separates good from evil. This separation, they thought, is the real freedom of the spirit. So how can a resurrected body, being evil, prove that Jesus was more than a man? The Resurrection was a stumblingblock to Greeks because they believed the body is evil. So both Jews and Greeks were troubled, defiant, and hostile.

However, some Jews and Greeks from Thessalonica and Beroea were converted. Paul later applauds their faith. "And you became imitators of us and of the Lord, for you received the word in much

from The Interpreter's Dictionary of the Bible
Copyright © 1962 by Abingdon Press

This lesson mentions Asia, Troas, Macedonia, and Athens. This map shows their location. Macedonia is the northern part of Greece and the southern part of Yugoslavia.

MACEDONIA AND GREECE

From The Interpreter's Dictionary of the Bible
Copyright © 1962 by Abingdon Press

This lesson mentions Philippi, Thessalonica, Beroea, and Achaia. This map shows their location. The area shown in this map is in modern Greece.

affliction, with joy inspired by the Holy Spirit; so that you became an example to all the believers in Macedonia and in Achaia." (1 Thessalonians 1:6-7)

CHRIST PRESENTED TO THE INTELLECTUAL CENTER OF THE WORLD
Acts 17:16-34

Leaving Timothy and Silas at Beroea, Paul went to Athens. In Paul's time, Athens was the intellectual center of the Roman Empire. For several centuries past, Athens had led the world in science and discovery. Many of the famous philosophers and educators of the ancient world had taught or studied in Athens. The people of Athens took great pride in their advanced learning. Athens was also the city where Socrates, Plato, and Aristotle had lived and taught. The Epicurean and Stoic philosophers still had much influence in Athens in Paul's time.

Undoubtedly, Paul was delighted to visit Athens. It was the most beautiful city in the Roman Empire. It had a score of temples, an altar to "an unknown god," colonnaded buildings, a library, Senate buildings, and the Acropolis. On the Acropolis was the world-famous Parthenon, which housed some of the most beautiful sculpture in the world. Just to the west of the Acropolis was a hill called Mars Hill, or Areopagus. (See map of Achaia on page 91.)

> **Now while Paul was waiting for them at Athens, his spirit was provoked within him as he saw that the city was full of idols . . . . And they took hold of him and brought him to the Areopagus, saying, "May we know what this new teaching is which you present?" (Acts 17:16, 19)**

Paul attacked at two points. (1) He "argued in the synagogue with the Jews and the devout persons." (2) He argued "in the market place every day with those who chanced to be there." In the market place were Epicurean and Stoic philosophers. Some said of Paul, "What would this babbler say?" The word *babbler* means literally "seed picker," that is, one who picks (as a pigeon) at small odds and ends. Others said he was "a preacher of foreign divinities."

So the philosophers "took hold of him and brought him to the Areopagus." The Areopagus was a hill (called Mars Hill) on which a lovely stone building stood. This building was the meeting place for the council on religious, moral, and philosophical affairs. This council had the power to give or to withhold license to a new teacher or philosopher. It had the authority to say who could teach in the market place.

So Paul faced the thirty members of this council. These thirty members were learned men. Most of them belonged either to the Stoic or to the Epicurean school of philosophy. Both schools were sincere and earnest. Both were concerned about virtue and how it could be obtained.

A few classic sayings of some of the Stoics will help us to realize the kind of men Paul faced. Epictetus wrote: "Friend . . . Dare to look up to God and say, 'Deal with me hence forth as thou wilt; thou and I are of one mind. I am thine; I refuse nothing that seems good to thee; lead where thou wilt. . . .' " This statement reminds us of Jesus' prayer, "Not my will, but thine be done." Speaking of prayer, the Stoic philosopher Seneca said that prayer is not a request to God but communion of the mind with God. He then defined true worship as first of all believing in the gods, then recognizing their majesty and goodness. He said that whoever imitates the gods has adequately worshiped them.

John Wesley admired another Stoic, Marcus Aurelius. In many ways the thoughts of the emperor Aurelius were like those of Paul. But Aurelius did not know Jesus Christ. Yet, Wesley claimed: "What a strange emperor! And what a strange heathen! Giving thanks to God for all the good things he enjoyed! . . . I make no doubt but this is one of those 'many' who 'shall come from the east and the west, and sit down with Abraham, Isaac, and Jacob,' while 'the children of the kingdom,' nominal Christians, are 'shut out.' "

The men Paul addressed were high-minded, virtuous men.

> **So Paul, standing in the middle of the Areopagus, said: "Men of Athens, I perceive that in every way you are very religious. For as I passed along, and observed the objects of your worship, I found also an altar with this inscription, 'To an unknown god.' What therefore you worship as unknown, this I proclaim to you." (Acts 17:22-23)**

Paul knew that many of the council members before him believed in one god. He spoke of "the unknown god" in order to get his ideas before them. Diogenes Laertius wrote that about 600 B.C. Athens faced a terrible pestilence. It could not be stopped. Epimenides, a Cretan poet, thought of a plan. He suggested letting a flock of sheep loose in the city of Athens.

If any lay down, they would be sacrificed to the nearest god. If a sheep lay down anywhere else, not near a shrine of a known deity, it would be sacrificed to "the unknown god." Altars inscribed to these unknown gods lined the roads near Athens. Paul had read them.

Paul's address to these learned men included the following points.

(1) There is but one God. Paul does not bother to argue against polytheism (many gods). Most of his audience would have agreed with him.

(2) God is the creator of heaven and earth. "In the beginning God. . . ." How foolish to think that God, who lived before the earth existed, lives now in manmade shrines.

(3) God does not need gifts from men, such as the blood of rams, which were sacrificed in Athens. God is not "served by human hands, as though he needed anything." God does not need gifts. Rather God gives gifts to men. He gives the gifts of "life and breath and everything."

(4) God "made from one every nation of men to live on all the

face of the earth." Alexander the Great was right in hoping for the unity of mankind. But this hope cannot be realized through war and conquest. Unity comes from the Creator of us all.

(5) Men are made to "seek God, in the hope that they might feel after him and find him." God makes men restless until they find their rest in him.

(6) God is not far from any of us. To make his point with these philosophers, Paul quoted a passage from the writing of the Greek poet, Epimenides: "In him we live and move and have our being."

(7) God is not dead, as some believed. He is a living God. Paul said that the days of "feeling after" God are over. The period of groping is over. Now men have a full revelation of God in Jesus Christ. Men no longer need to have adolescent ideas about God. They need to grow religiously. At another time Paul explained this idea to the Corinthian churches. "When I was a child, I spoke like a child, I thought like a child, I reasoned like a child; when I became a man, I gave up childish ways." (1 Corinthians 13:11) Growth in understanding God is a lifetime job. A reasonable man has a responsibility to grow.

(8) The final proof of this revelation of God in and through Jesus Christ is the fact that God raised him from the dead. (Acts 17:31)

As is always the case, "some mocked; but others said, 'We will hear you again about this.'" Another response was "some men joined him and believed, among them Dionysius the Areopagite and a woman named Damaris and others with them."

11. God's People in Corinth
(Acts 18:1 through 19:20)

Paul left Athens dejected. In Athens he had appealed to men at the intellectual center of the Roman Empire. But he had not founded a church. How he must have suffered. He could not interest Athenians in the Christ who meant more to him than life.

From a city of learning, Athens, Paul went to a city of vice, Corinth. Strangely, the barriers of vice were not as hard to overcome as the barriers of intellectual pride. Great things happened in Corinth. For an account of these events, read Acts 18:1 through 19:20. This portion of Scripture ends the fifth section of Acts. This fifth section tells how the church moved into Europe.

THE GOSPEL PREACHED AT THE CAPITAL OF ACHAIA
Acts 18:1-4

> After this he left Athens and went to Corinth. And he found a Jew named Aquila, a native of Pontus, lately come from Italy with his wife Priscilla. . . . (Acts 18:1-2)

Paul left Athens a despondent man. He arrived at Corinth a sick man. Later in a letter to Corinth, he says: "I was with you in weakness and in much fear and trembling." (1 Corinthians 2:3) His fatigue and sorrow must have stirred up the thorn in his flesh. Apparently Luke was not with Paul at this time. Luke and Paul met next in Philippi. (See Acts 20:6.) How Paul must have yearned for his medical companion during these many months.

Corinth became a significant city for Paul. Over the years, he visited Corinth three times. He wrote four letters to its churches. From Corinth he wrote several other letters, for example, one to Thessalonica and one to Rome.

Yet Corinth was an unlikely place to begin a church of Jesus Christ. Let's take an imaginary walk through Corinth as it was in the days of Paul. We will try to see this great commercial city through his eyes.

First, let us locate Corinth. (Refer to the map on page 91.) It is about thirty miles due west of Athens. Leaving Athens we would cross the isthmus (a kind of land-bridge) to the Peloponnesus. Cor-

The Apostle Paul
Rembrandt van Ryn
The National Gallery of Art, Washington, D. C.
Widener Collection

This portrait of Paul shows him writing one of his letters.

inth is located just south of the isthmus, and in between two sea harbors: Lechaeum on the west and Cenchreae on the east. Each year slaves and animals pulled hundreds of boats overland from one harbor to the other. This was a distance of about four miles. If they were not pulled overland, the boats had to sail in rough waters for several weeks to go from Lechaeum to Cenchreae.

We take our imaginary tour of Corinth by starting in the north. (See the map on page 92.) We walk south down the main street, called Lechaion Road. This road begins at the harbor of Lechaeum and stretches southward into Corinth. We walk only about two hundred feet before we see on the left the synagogue where Crispus was the chief officer. Next door to the synagogue is the house of Justus, where Paul lived. Within a block, we look to our right (west) to see the Basilica, an oblong building where the Roman governor had his office. Two hundred feet farther west is the Temple of Apollo, which was six hundred years old in Paul's time. It was built at the same time as the Parthenon in Athens. Continuing south on the Lechaion Road, we soon enter the market place. The market place is bounded by scores of lovely marble shops shaded by graceful columns. Many of these shops have marble gutters and mosaic floors.

In the center of the market place is the raised platform (tribunal). Here Gallio the governor held court. Here some Corinthians sought to have Paul tried. Less than two hundred feet east of the market place is the famous sacred Peirenian Spring. The spring had six low, square, cavelike chambers from which water flowed to an open-air fountain. Then the water flowed southeast into four long reservoirs. Each reservoir contained about 150,000 gallons of water. The cool water supplied an elaborate cooling system for the shops on the southern side of the market place. Just south of this shopping area was the largest secular building in all Greece. It housed thirty-three night clubs. Here the sailors whose boats were being hauled overland spent their nights in drunken brawling and prostitution.

In the far south, on a high hill, was the truly magnificent Temple of Aphrodite. Attached to this temple were one thousand religious prostitutes ("saints" of Venus). They plied their trade in the name of religion in the thirty-three taverns and in the market place at evening. Of course, Paul was horrified at this sexual vice. And he knew that their "worship" was high blasphemy. They surely were a people in need of the gospel.

To this beautiful yet sordid city the dejected and sick Paul came. Perhaps it was just what he needed. He who lives by spiritual values may be encouraged when he sees the bitter fruits of sensuality and idolatry. He may be spurred to action.

AT FIRST CHURCH, CORINTH
Acts 18:5-11

> And he [Paul] left there and went to the house of a man named Titius Justus, a worshiper of God; his house was next door to the synagogue. Crispus, the ruler of the synagogue, believed in the Lord, together with all his household; and many of the Corinthians hearing Paul believed and were baptized. (Acts 18:7-8)

Paul and Aquila met in Corinth. Both were Christian Jews. Both were refugees. Aquila was forced to leave Rome (A.D. 49) when the emperor Claudius ordered all Jews to leave the capital city. Paul had been forced to leave a number of cities of Macedonia. Both men were well-born. Both were tentmakers (weavers of goat hair) and leather workers. It was fortunate for Paul that he met Aquila and Priscilla. They helped bring Paul back to his old self, lifting his morale both physically and spiritually. In no time at all Paul was back in the synagogue, preaching. But soon the Jews opposed him, and he left the synagogue in anger. Apparently Paul left the comforts of the home of Aquila and Priscilla because he wanted to be completely with and for the Gentiles. He moved next door to the synagogue with a Gentile, Titius Justus. Justus was a friend of the synagogue and a worshiper of God.

Paul's first convert was his next-door neighbor, Crispus, the chief officer of the synagogue he had just left. What a rumor that must have stirred up in the Jewish congregation! Soon a Christian congregation was meeting at the home of Justus. Consider the people who came to this house-church for fellowship. Some of them were Jews such as Crispus, Paul, Aquila and Priscilla, Timothy and Silas, Erastus, and eventually Sosthenes. (See 1 Corinthians 1:1.) Others were Greeks such as Gaius, Stephanas, Fortunatus, Chloe and her family, and Achaicus. What a cosmopolitan group that was. What a wonderful experience they had combining ideas. Each person of each nationality interpreted the good news from his own point of view based on his own background. What a spirit of openness to a variety of ideas and personalities this congregation had. And what a team they must have been as they witnessed in the market place to those who were caught in the drunkenness and depravity of Corinth.

Who were these converts? Some were city fathers like Erastus. But others were not so well placed or well known. Paul lists some of their sins: immorality, idolatry, adultery, sexual perversions, thievery, greed, robbery. "And such were some of you," he admits. But he quickly affirms their changed lives. "But you were washed, you were sanctified, you were justified in the name of the Lord Jesus Christ and in the Spirit of our God." (See 1 Corinthians 6:9-11.)

What kind of church would that be, we wonder. It was the kind of church that Paul could write to with love and appreciation. Changed men, twice-born men, were the hallmarks of Christian faith.

> **And the Lord said to Paul one night in a vision, "Do not be afraid, but speak and do not be silent; for I am with you, and no man shall attack you to harm you; for I have many people in this city." (Acts 18:9-10)**

In Corinth Paul had a vision, a private revelation. Just as the Lord revealed himself to Peter at the home of Simon, an unworthy tanner, so he revealed himself to Paul in the home of Justus, a Gentile.

The experience contained four key parts. (1) The risen Lord appeared to Paul. "And the Lord said to Paul. . . ." This was Paul's private religious experience. No one else saw the Lord or heard the voice. The risen Christ was with Paul and was counseling him. Jesus had promised, "I will pray the Father, and he will give you another Counselor, to be with you for ever." (John 14:16) Jesus carried out his promise by coming to Paul as a divine counselor.

(2) The Lord calmed Paul's fears of conflict in the market place. "Do not be afraid, but speak and do not be silent." Courage and confidence are not based on human strength. They are based on the assurance of God's presence: I am with you always.

(3) The presence of Christ gave Paul power. The challenge, "Do not be afraid, but speak," and the promise, "I am with you," were not new to Paul. Paul had read the words of the prophets. Now once again he heard the word of God for himself.

Jeremiah, who had written six hundred years earlier, was one of Paul's favorite prophets. Paul preached that Jeremiah's prophecies were fulfilled in Jesus. Through Jeremiah God said, a new covenant will I give—one written, not on tablets of stone, but in the hearts (thought-lives) of men. Jesus identified his own life with this new covenant. "The blood of the new covenant" became the lifeblood of the new Israel, the church of Christ.

But Paul, in his turmoil, remembered also Jeremiah's early fears and doubts. At the time God called him, Jeremiah cried out:

> **"Ah, Lord God! Behold, I do not know how to speak, for I am only a youth." But the Lord said to me,**
> **"Do not say, 'I am only a youth';**
> **for to all to whom I send you you shall go,**
> **and whatever I command you you shall speak.**
> **Be not afraid of them,**
> **for I am with you to deliver you, says the Lord." (Jeremiah 1:6-8)**

God gave Paul a similar promise at Corinth. (a) Speak up. (b)

Do not be afraid. (c) I am with you. Where had Jeremiah first heard these words? Many times in his youth he had heard of Joshua, who was called by Moses to lead Israel. Moses, in front of all the people, said to Joshua: "Be strong and of good courage; . . . It is the Lord who goes before you; he will be with you, he will not fail you or forsake you; do not fear or be dismayed." (Deuteronomy 31:7-8)

And how could Moses be so sure? He himself had that same divine promise and fulfillment in his life. At the foot of Mount Sinai he met God in the burning bush. He asked God to identify himself. "Tell me your name, Lord," Moses said. Instead, God told Moses what he

This lesson mentions Achaia and Corinth. This map shows their location.

From *The Interpreter's Dictionary of the Bible*
Copyright © 1962 by Abingdon Press

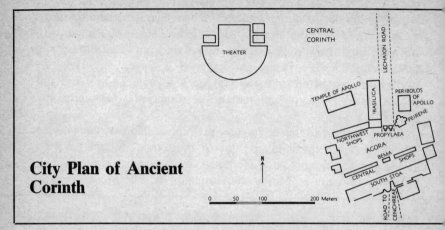

City Plan of Ancient Corinth

would do. I will be with you! I, the Lord, am and will be with you. (This is what Exodus 3:13-15 means. The Hebrew verb is generally translated "I am," but is more correctly translated "I will be.") The promise is: I, the Lord your God, will be with you as you need me. Moses knew the power of this promise. Joshua conquered portions of the promised land under this assurance. David started a new dynasty with this blessing. Jeremiah was confident of a new covenant fulfilling this promise.

So Paul heard the same promise at Corinth. Be not afraid. I, the Lord, am with you. Paul remembered that Jesus said: God "will give you another Counselor, *to be with you for ever,* even the Spirit of truth, . . . you know him, for *he dwells with you,* and *will be in you.*" (John 14:16-17, italics added)

This is the meaning of the strangely warmed heart. We do not walk alone. God is with us. *In this experience we find the unity of the Old and New Testaments.* The Lord is and ever will be with us. Emmanuel!

(4) "I have many people in this city." Paul may have recalled Jonah's hatred for the wicked city of Nineveh. Jonah discovered that God wanted the hated enemies to be converted, for God loved them. Paul discovered that God had many people in Corinth. Some of them were drunkards and prostitutes. Some of them were jealous persons. Some knew no purpose for their lives. But they all were objects of God's love. Paul knew that all persons need the new life that the gospel offers. Facing the reality of God's love for all persons is the heart of Christlike living. Later Paul wrote this in one of his letters to Corinth. (1 Corinthians 13)

What a tremendous power Christian experience is. On the strength of this vision Paul "stayed a year and six months, teaching the word of God among them." (Acts 18:11)

We may use four key words to describe Paul's experience. These four words are *Scripture, tradition, experience,* and *reason.* (1) *Scripture* supported Paul's belief that the Lord is a living God and that he does show his will to men. This is the witness of Moses, Elijah, Nathan, Amos, Isaiah, Jeremiah, and Paul. (2) *Tradition,* both Jewish and Greek, claimed that God guides men. Even Socrates, the famous Gentile philosopher, claimed that God kindled his mind with divinely inspired ideas. The oral, as well as written, tradition of the Jews supported Paul's belief in the guidance of the Lord. (3) *Experience* argued that God lives, loves us, is with us, and guides us. The Lord had been with Paul when he was stoned and when he was in prison. He had stayed with Paul when hostile Jews rejected him. And God would be with him as he faced the wickedness and degradation of Corinth. (4) Paul must have *reasoned,* as he had in Athens, that God makes all men to "feel after him and find him." (Acts 17:27) God loved the immoral Corinthians too. And they needed to learn to love and care too. It is *reasonable* to assume that lost souls really want a ray of hope to light the darkness of their spiritual dungeons. They need and want freedom, though often they do not know it. Men are made for spiritual values, for love, justice, truth, mercy, and kindness. Men are made for doing whatever shows kinship to God.

Paul could not have left Corinth now without denying his Lord. We need to ask what our Corinths are. Where do we feel God wants us to take our stand in our day? Where should we speak out, unafraid, because He is with us and because all people are His people?

GALLIO, PAUL, SOSTHENES
Acts 18:12-23

> But when Gallio was proconsul of Achaia, the Jews made a united attack upon Paul. . . . Gallio said to the Jews, ". . . since it is a matter of questions about words and names and your own law, see to it yourselves; I refuse to be a judge of these things." (Acts 18:12, 14, 15)

Gallio became proconsul of Achaia in A.D. 51-52. *Achaia* is an ancient word for southern Greece. Paul was already a minister to Corinth when Gallio arrived. Some Jews (loyal to Judaism) brought suit against Paul, saying, "This man is persuading men to worship

God contrary to the law." (Acts 18:13) They may have thought that the first days of Gallio's rule would be a good time to get rid of Paul. Paul was ready to defend himself. But Gallio dismissed the case.

Why did Gallio dismiss the case? When we realize who he was, we may understand better. He was the elder brother of the Stoic philosopher Seneca. Seneca believed in God. He felt that rituals and rites were inferior ways to worship God. Seneca stated that the best way to pray is to seek communion with the mind of God. That is, the person who seeks the purposes of God and makes them his own prays best.

Would Gallio have supported his brother's ideas? What kind of man was Gallio? Seneca claimed that Gallio was "the noblest Roman of them all." He said that no one could be as kind to a friend as Gallio was to everybody and that he deserved the greatest affection. So Gallio was more than a public official. He must have loved what his brother also loved—courage, a disciplined temper, noble ideas of God, and the virtuous life.

When Gallio noted that the dispute in Corinth was merely over words, he knew that jealousy alone moved the Jews. Surely Gallio had learned as a boy, when he and his philosopher brother talked together, that openness toward new ideas is essential to growth. Gallio did not see openness toward the ideas of others in these Jews. So he dismissed the case. The Gentiles who were present beat Sosthenes, the chief official of the synagogue. Paul surely must have thought of Stephen's stoning. We wonder what he said and did. Something great must have happened, because we learn that Sosthenes, the ruler of the synagogue, was converted. He became one of Paul's companions. (See 1 Corinthians 1:1. What a story lies behind this simple phrase. We wish Luke had told us more about Sosthenes.)

Spring, the time for the Passover, was near. Paul wanted to observe Passover in Jerusalem. So he left Corinth. He visited briefly in Ephesus and Caesarea. He worshiped in Jerusalem. Then he returned to Syrian Antioch to report about his experiences.

Paul soon was ready to travel again. He began this third missionary journey by going to Ephesus.

THE ELOQUENT PREACHER FROM EGYPT
Acts 18:24-28

Now a Jew named Apollos, a native of Alexandria, came to Ephesus. He was an eloquent man, well versed in the scriptures. (Acts 18:24)

Apollos was a successful Christian missionary from Alexandria in Egypt. Alexandria was the home of the Jewish philosopher Philo.

There Apollos had learned a new method of studying the Bible. Philo taught that you should read every verse literally for what it has to say, and that each verse had further meanings also. Each word or term may have a hidden or double meaning. Augustine read the New Testament in the same way that Philo taught Apollos to read the Old Testament. For example, Augustine read the familiar sentence *A certain man was going down from Jerusalem to Jericho.* But Augustine claimed that many of the words had a hidden meaning. So, "a certain man" meant Adam. "Jerusalem" meant the heavenly city of peace from which Adam was expelled. "Jericho" meant the moon, the symbol of man's mortality. This way of reading the Bible is called "allegorizing." This practice is usually an abuse of Scripture. But some great men have read hidden meanings into the Scriptures.

Apollos from Alexandria was "an eloquent man, well versed in the scriptures." (Acts 18:24) His style of interpreting Scripture and his style of preaching differed greatly from Paul's. This difference caused divisions among the Christians in Corinth and Ephesus. Paul's approach was to interpret the Old Testament as prophecies and promises now fulfilled in the person of Jesus Christ. Apollos' method was to allegorize. When "Priscilla and Aquila heard him, they took him and expounded to him the way of God more accurately." (Acts 18:26)

Later Apollos decided to go to Corinth. Aquila and Priscilla wrote a letter of confidence to introduce him to the Corinthian disciples. Though Apollos interpreted Scripture differently, he was accepted as a fellow missionary, "showing by the scriptures that the Christ was Jesus." (Acts 18:28)

NEW SETTINGS IN ASIA MINOR
Acts 19:1-20

And he entered the synagogue . . . some were stubborn and disbelieved . . . . he withdrew from them, taking the disciples with him, and argued daily in the hall of Tyrannus. (Acts 19:8-9)

Paul was more open to change than many persons realize. When the Jews in Ephesus closed their synagogues to him, he rented a lecture room in the school of Tyrannus. He lectured there for two years. And he had amazing success. "All the residents of Asia heard the word of the Lord, both Jews and Greeks." (Acts 19:10) Some persons were converted from magic. Read the account of the great bonfire of magic scrolls and books. (Acts 19:13-20)

The fifth section of Acts ends at Acts 19:20. This story of how the church moved through Europe ends triumphantly. "So the word of the Lord grew and prevailed mightily." (Acts 19:20)

12. The Way to Jerusalem
(Acts 19:21 through 23:35)

The Acts of the Apostles reaches its high point as Paul takes the gospel to Rome. Paul had been God's witness before religious and political leaders in Jerusalem, Palestine, Syria, Cyprus, Asia Minor, and Greece. Now he prepared to take the gospel to Rome, perhaps to Caesar himself. But first he took a collection of money from many churches to the mother church in Jerusalem. He foresaw his arrest and his need to appeal to Caesar. Rome was the goal toward which Paul moved.

We have seen that Acts is divided into six parts. (1) Acts 1:1 through 6:7 tells of the church in Jerusalem. (2) Acts 6:8 through 9:31 tells how the church moved through Palestine. (3) Acts 9:32 through 12:24 tells how the church spread to Antioch of Syria. (4) Acts 12:25 through 16:5 tells how the church reached Asia Minor. (5) Acts 16:6 through 19:20 tells of the expansion of the church into Europe. (6) Acts 19:21 through 28:31 tells of the expansion of the church to Rome.

Before you begin this lesson, read Acts 19:21 through 23:35. In this section you will read of Paul's last visit to Jerusalem, his arrest, and his witness under extreme circumstances.

LIFE AT EPHESUS
Acts 19:21-22

Now after these events Paul resolved in the Spirit to pass through Macedonia and Achaia and go to Jerusalem, saying, "After I have been there, I must also see Rome.". . . he himself stayed in Asia for a while.

Ephesus was the capital of the Roman province Asia. The word *Asia* here refers to the southwestern coastal area of Asia Minor. Ephesus was the racial melting pot of Asia. The city was one of the four greatest cities of the Roman Empire. The other three were Rome, Antioch in Syria, and Alexandria in Egypt.

Ephesus was a travel and trade center between East and West. It lay between the great sea lanes and four main highways into Asia Minor. Sailors, merchants, and scholars from throughout the Roman Empire mingled in Ephesus. This complex, worldly city was a trade center of the empire. It was also a battlefield for religion. In 560 B.C. King Croesus of Lydia conquered Ephesus and introduced a Lydian fertility goddess. The worship of a fertility goddess was the chief religion in Ephesus for many centuries. The Greeks called her Artemis. The Romans called her Diana. Her religion dominated the life of Ephesus, with its legalized prostitution and its great temple.

Another god, Mithra, sought a place in Ephesus too. Mithra was son of the sun god. Worship of Mithra included baptism in the blood of a bull for the remission of sins, a communion meal of bread and wine, and the hope of immortal life. Mithraism competed with Christianity throughout the Empire.

Besides Artemis and Mithra, the emperor was worshiped. The officials of the state religion of Rome were called Asiarchs. The responsibility of an Asiarch, as in Ephesus, was to supervise the imperial religious festivals and to see that the people worshiped the emperor. A good account of this is found in Revelation 13:11-18. There the second beast refers to the Asiarchs who forced persons to bow down and worship the image of the emperor.

WHEN MEN BECOME BEASTS
Acts 19:23-41

> **About that time there arose no little stir concerning the Way. For a man named Demetrius, a silversmith, who made silver shrines of Artemis, brought no little business to the craftsmen. . . .**
>
> **". . . there is danger not only that this trade of ours may come into disrepute but also that the temple of the great goddess Artemis may count for nothing, and that she may even be deposed from her magnificence, she whom all Asia and the world worship."** (Acts 19:23-24, 27)

The temple of Artemis was one of the seven wonders of the ancient world. It was 340 feet long and 160 feet wide. It had one hundred marble pillars, each sixty feet high. Eight of these huge pillars are still being used in the famous Blue Mosque of Istanbul. The marble blocks of the temple were cemented with gold instead of mortar. The inner sanctuary was seventy feet wide and open to the skies. This inner sanctuary contained a great stone image of the goddess Artemis that had "fallen from the skies." This image had been carved from a meteorite five feet long.

In this part of Acts, Luke describes a near-riot in Ephesus. In that scene Luke describes several persons. (1) *Demetrius and the*

This picture shows Paul's determination as he returns to Jerusalem for the last time.

---

silversmiths were concerned about their pocketbooks. They probably sold small images of Artemis for women to wear. Undoubtedly, they also sold some small images of the beautiful temple. Since the city was a thriving trade center, the search for souvenirs was great. (2) Paul's friends, *Gaius and Aristarchus,* were dragged into the 25,000-seat theater to explain the rejection of Artemis by the Christians. (3) *Alexander* was the spokesman put forward by the Jews. (4) The *town clerk* was the city official who presided over the Ephesian assemblies. He kept public records and introduced the agenda for the meetings of the assemblies. It was his responsibility to keep the peace in Ephesus. So when he heard the angry shouts, he tried to calm the mob. Finally he got them to listen to him. (5) The *Asiarchs* were priests of the imperial worship of Caesar.

Interestingly enough, the Asiarchs supported Paul. Why did they? Apparently they supported Paul because he was making inroads into the cult of Artemis. The Asiarchs had tried to do this and had failed. So they supported Paul, who offered a way of worship that might cut into the worship of Artemis.

The rioters in the theater soon calmed down under orders from the town clerk. But jealousy and economic fear had done their work. Luke described the emotional fury of that hour. "Now some cried one thing, some another; for the assembly was in confusion, and most of them did not know why they had come together." (Acts 19:32) This was a typical mob scene. Reason gave way to prejudices. At times prejudice becomes so strong that it rules men's lives. Good and rational men may then become beasts. Religious and racial bigotry are sometimes that strong. Racism may have been a sore point in Ephesus. Perhaps the dark-skinned Jews and the light-skinned Ephesians doubted each other's motives.

But the riot cramped Paul's freedom to teach in the school of Tyrannus. (See Acts 19:9.) Because his work stopped for the present, he prepared to leave Ephesus. Later Paul said that his work there

Ralph McDonald

had not been very successful. "You are aware that all who are in Asia turned away from me." (2 Timothy 1:15)

Several things happened during Paul's stay in Ephesus that Luke did not mention. Paul was imprisoned with Andronicus and Junias. (See Romans 16:7.) He fought with beasts in the theater at Ephesus. (See 1 Corinthians 15:32.) Prisca (Priscilla) and Aquila saved Paul from some terrible, unidentified peril in Ephesus. They "risked their necks for my life." (Romans 16:3-4)

From a worldly point of view, you might say Paul was a failure. He had to leave Ephesus. He could not lecture in the hall of Tyrannus because of Demetrius' charges. But from the point of view of spiritual values, Paul was a success. Scores of persons found new life, new hope, and a new unity with persons of other races through faith in Christ. These spiritual values of hope, love, mercy, and justice were far superior to the worldly values of the Ephesians. God judges a person's success by spiritual, not worldly, values.

RETURN TO THE MOTHER CHURCH AT JERUSALEM

When Paul left Ephesus, he went back to Corinth for a brief visit. At this time he wrote his Letter to the Romans. This book has led to the conversion of thousands of persons, including great Christians like Augustine, Martin Luther, and John Wesley. The message of Romans is the simple but profound claim of Paul: Men are justified by grace through faith in Jesus Christ. By no other means do men find salvation. A man is saved by the grace of God as granted in Christ Jesus. He is not saved by doing good deeds.

When Paul left Corinth, he passed through Philippi. He was warmed to have Luke join him again. It seems likely that Luke had been working as a doctor in Philippi for these two and one half years. While he was at Philippi, Paul wrote several letters to Corinth. One of these is 2 Corinthians 1 through 7, a letter of relief and joy at his good visit with them. The other letter is 2 Corinthians 8 and 9, which was taken to Corinth by Titus and Luke, "the brother who is famous among all the churches." (2 Corinthians 8:18)

From Philippi, the company went on to Troas. They stayed there for a week. The service at Troas is the first reference in the New Testament to a Sunday service.

On the first day of the week, when we were gathered together to break bread, Paul talked with them. . . .

But going ahead to the ship, we set sail for Assos, intending to take Paul aboard there; for so he had arranged, intending himself to go by land. (Acts 20:7, 13)

Paul decided to walk alone from Troas to Assos. There he would meet the others of his company, who had gone in the boat. He wanted to be alone with Christ. Jesus had often withdrawn from the crowd to be alone with God. Paul, like Jesus, faced a dark future. His face too was set toward Jerusalem. His friends would try to keep him from doing what he knew he must do. He felt he had to go to Jerusalem one more time. He knew the danger. So he thought and prayed about his future, that it might fit in with God's will.

At Miletus Paul sent for the elders of the church of Ephesus to come to him. He spoke to them in farewell tones.

"You yourselves know how I lived among you all the time from the first day that I set foot in Asia, serving the Lord with all humility and with tears and with trials which befell me through the plots of the Jews; how I did not shrink from declaring to you anything that was profitable, and teaching you in public and from house to house. . . ." (Acts 20:18b-20)

Acts 20:18-35 is Paul's farewell speech as he leaves Asia Minor. In this speech we have a summary picture of Paul, the great apostle.

Paul's love shines through this last talk with the Ephesian elders. (1) He reminded the elders of the past. He reminded them that he had served the Lord with humility. His service showed his concern for persons. He had told the truth. He had always taught that which was for the good of others. He had not diluted the truth in order to make it easy or pleasant. He had preached that men might repent before God and gain faith in Jesus Christ. (2) Paul admitted that his future was dark and uncertain. Yet he felt "bound in the Spirit." He was certain that Christ wanted him in Jerusalem. There he would go regardless of cost. Here, as elsewhere in Acts, the Spirit guides Paul directly. (3) Paul asked the overseers of the church to "care for the church of God." (Acts 20:28) (4) Then he commended them to God who is able to give them "the inheritance among all those who are sanctified." (Acts 20:32) This statement reminds us of Jesus' promise, "Blessed are the poor in spirit, for theirs is the kingdom of heaven." (Matthew 5:3) What an inheritance!

When he left Miletus, Paul took a boat to Patara. He and the company caught another boat there and made their way to Caesarea, visiting other towns along the way. In Caesarea, they stayed in the home of Philip the evangelist, who was one of the seven. (See Acts 21:8.) While at Caesarea, Paul spoke clearly of his willingness to suffer for Christ. No pleading by friends could turn aside his will to follow the Spirit to Jerusalem. After a brief visit, Paul went to Jerusalem.

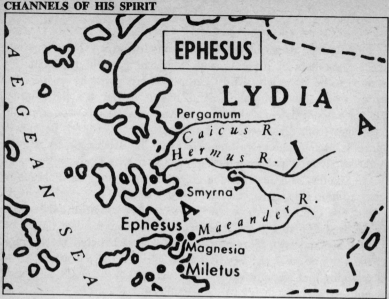

From *The Interpreter's Dictionary of the Bible*
Copyright © 1962 by Abingdon Press

A TIME FOR COMPROMISE
Acts 21:15 through 22:30

> On the following day Paul went in with us to James; and all the elders were present. After greeting them, he related one by one the things that God had done among the Gentiles through his ministry. And when they heard it, they glorified God. (Acts 21: 18-20)

Several things took place when Paul arrived in Jerusalem. (1) Paul and the other delegates (Acts 20:4) delivered their gifts to the mother church. No apostles were present. Only the elders and James, the brother of Jesus, were there. Strangely, Luke does not refer to how the church received Paul's offering. (See 2 Corinthians 8:1 through 9:15 for the story of Paul's collection for the poor in Jerusalem.) (2) The delegates told the elders of God's success through Paul among Gentiles. (3) James, the brother of Jesus, recommended that Paul show his loyalty to Judaism. James, himself a former Pharisee, knew that Paul made the law second to faith. But James also knew that some Jews in Jerusalem were ready to kill Paul if he did not make clear that he was loyal to Judaism. And Paul did see his Christian faith as fulfilling Judaism. He did not wish to replace Judaism. He wished to complete it. So he agreed to James's suggestion to make a religious vow and to finance four other men in a similar vow. These actions would show his loyalty to the law and his obedience to the requirements of the temple.

> This lesson mentions Ephesus and Miletus. This map shows their location. The area shown in this map is in modern Turkey.

The fulfillment of his vow had several parts. (1) Paul must not drink wine or eat meat for thirty days. (2) He must let his hair grow for a month and then offer it on the altar. (3) He must spend the last seven of the thirty days in the temple courts. (4) He must pay for the sacrifices of the four men—a lamb, a ram, unleavened bread, cakes, and a cereal offering.

In fulfilling these vows, Paul adjusted his own normal practice. He knew that such ritual acts are not needed for salvation. Man is saved not by deeds or vows but by the grace of God.

Paul knew that a compromise for the sake of others may be better than rigid opinions. He weighed the merits of each side. (1) He could refuse to obey the law and be considered an unfaithful Jew. (2) He could make and fulfill a vow that required obedience to certain acts in the temple. This way he could prove his loyalty to Judaism. For him, compromise did not mean selling out his Christian values for lesser values. Compromise was simply charity seeking its way in a thorny situation. Paul compromised because he realized that greater values lay in charitable actions than in rigid personal preferences.

Paul hoped that his vow would show his loyalty to the temple and to the Jewish faith. His hope was fruitless.

> **"Men of Israel, help! This is the man who is teaching men everywhere against the people and the law and this place; moreover he also brought Greeks into the temple, and he has defiled this holy place." (Acts 21:28)**

Some Jews from Asia were in the temple. They recognized Paul. They accused him of three things. (1) He destroys the law. (2) He insults the chosen people. (3) He defiles the temple. All these accusations were false.

Basically, these Jews thought that if the temple were opened to Gentiles, the status of the Jews as a chosen people would end. So separatism was the answer. They must keep Gentiles in their place. And their place was outside the temple. Only Jews belonged inside.

A mob formed quickly. Soon Paul was arrested by the Roman tribune. The tribune allowed Paul to speak to the mob that wanted his death. The mob listened until Paul claimed that God himself appeared in the temple to send Paul on a mission to the Gentiles. (See Acts 22:17-21.)

The tribune protected Paul and later brought him before the Sanhedrin for a hearing.

PAUL'S DEFENSE BEFORE THE SANHEDRIN
Acts 23:1-35

> **And Paul, looking intently at the council, said, "Brethren, I have lived before God in all good conscience up to this day." (Acts 23:1)**

The council (Sanhedrin) expected Paul to begin with the phrase *Rulers of the people and elders of Israel*. But he began with a word that showed religious equality—*brethren*. Because Paul did not show him the respect he thought he should have, Ananias, the chief priest, ordered Paul to be slapped. Then Paul lost his temper. He knew the law: "He who strikes the cheek of an Israelite, strikes, as it were, the glory of God." Paul was furious that the chief priest himself broke the law, especially since Paul was on trial himself for breaking the law. So Paul retorted sharply: You hypocrite! You pretend to love the law but violate it yourself! What kind of a judge of a court are you? Apparently Paul did not recognize Ananias. He did not know he was speaking to the high priest. But he did not really apologize for what he had said.

Paul found a way out of his difficulty. He got the two religious factions, Pharisees and Sadducees, to argue with each other in the Sanhedrin. The Pharisees believed in resurrection. The Sadducees did not. So Paul claimed that his case was really based on his hope in the resurrection, which he as a Pharisee believed. The Sanhedrin immediately split into two groups. A near riot ensued. Claudius Lysias, the Roman tribune, rescued Paul from the shouting, angry Sanhedrin.

That night, still under guard, Paul saw the Lord again.

> **The following night the Lord stood by him and said, "Take courage, for as you have testified about me at Jerusalem, so you must bear witness also at Rome." (Acts 23:11)**

Again the promise that God made to Moses, Joshua, David, and many others is made to Paul. I, the Lord, am with you. Be of good courage. Paul is clearly a part of the ancient covenant—the covenant of Emmanuel. God was with him. And Paul's life after his conversion was a personal declaration that God's promise is reliable.

13. The Final Trial
(Acts 24:1 through 28:31)

Paul tried his best to win Jews to Christ. Luke makes this clear. In every city Paul visited in the Roman Empire, he spoke first to Jews. Only when they turned him out did he go to the Gentiles. Paul saw good in this Jewish reaction. He hated to leave his fellow Jews, but he was convinced that taking the gospel to the Gentiles was God's way. Did not God say long ago that Israel would become a light to the Gentiles? And Paul saw himself as the instrument of that light.

Acts tells of six stages in the growth of the church, as we already have noted. The church (1) begins in Jerusalem, (2) expands through Palestine, (3) goes to Antioch, (4) spreads to Asia Minor and Galatia, (5) reaches Europe and finally (6) arrives in Rome. In this last part of Acts, Luke shows how the gospel reached Rome.

Luke says that Paul "lived there [Rome] two whole years at his own expense, and welcomed all who came to him, preaching the kingdom of God and teaching about the Lord Jesus Christ quite openly and unhindered." (Acts 28:30-31)

The last verses of the Gospel of Luke were fulfilled. Those verses say that repentance and forgiveness of sins should be preached in Jesus' name to all nations, beginning from Jerusalem and going eventually to Rome. (See Luke 24:47.)

Theophilus, who may have been an important man in Rome, would have liked Luke's record of the gospel, with its lowly origins in Palestine and its final appeal to imperial Rome.

Before you go on with this lesson, read Acts 24:1 through 28:31.

A ROMAN LAWYER, CHIEF PRIEST, SLAVE, CHRISTIAN
Acts 24:1-27

Acts 24 deals with two scenes. One is a court case. The other is a royal family scene.

In the first scene (Acts 24:1-23) the Roman lawyer Tertullus and Paul faced Felix, the Procurator of Judea. Tertullus was hired by Ananias, the high priest. He brought three charges against Paul.

He said that (1) Paul was an agitator. (2) Paul was a ringleader of the Nazarenes. False messianic leaders caused disorder on many occasions. Paul was tagged as one of those troublers of Rome in Israel. (3) Paul polluted the temple. Tertullus claimed that Paul had brought a Gentile into the temple in Jerusalem.

All three charges were false. Paul defended himself well. (1) He said that his motive in going to Jerusalem was a religious one. He went to worship God, not to stir up Jews. (2) Paul denied the claim that he went to the temple to cause conflict. The accusers had no witnesses to support this claim against him. (3) Paul stated that "according to the Way" he was worshiping God:

> **But this I admit to you, that according to the Way, which they call a sect, I worship the God of our fathers, believing everything laid down by the law or written in the prophets, having a hope in God which these themselves accept, that there will be a resurrection of both the just and the unjust. So I always take pains to have a clear conscience toward God and toward men. (Acts 24:14-16)**

Paul identified himself with Judaism by saying that he worshiped "the God of our fathers." He told Ananias, his accuser, that they were both sons of Abraham. They were both heirs of the covenant that God had made with Israel long ago. As a Christian Paul went one step further than the high priest. He said that the blessing all mankind was to receive from Abraham's decendants had become a reality in Jesus Christ. He claimed to believe in the same law and in the same prophets as other Pharisees. He argued that he was not really on trial for the three charges made by the Roman lawyer, but for having a hope in God based on the resurrection of Jesus the Christ.

We should act as Paul did under stress. Not once did he turn sour or act bitterly toward his religious elders. He simply bore witness to his faith. How simple. How profound. He asked them to open their minds toward his religious experience. He had seen and heard the risen Christ. He wanted those who believed in Judaism to see that Christ fulfilled their hopes.

Felix could find no validity to Tertullus' charges. So he postponed judgment. He said that he would decide the case when Lysias the Roman tribune came from Jersualem. (Lysias had rescued Paul in Jerusalem and had written a letter to Felix. See Acts 23:23-30.)

The second scene in Acts 24 was in the royal palace, with Felix and his wife Drusilla, who agreed to hear Paul. Drusilla was a Jewess. Felix wanted her opinion about Paul.

Who were Felix and Drusilla? Felix had been a slave. He was the first slave in history to become a governor of a Roman province. His brother Pallas, a favorite of the emperor Nero, had requested and secured his brother's freedom. Felix was without scruples. He was capable of hiring thugs to murder his closest supporters.

Felix had been married three times. (1) His first wife is unknown. (2) His second wife was the granddaughter of Marc Anthony and Cleopatra. (3) His third wife was Drusilla. Her father was King Herod Agrippa I, who killed James the son of Zebedee. (See Acts 12:1-2.) Drusilla had been married to the King of Emessa, but she had left him at Felix's request.

This event is described in Acts 28:1-6.

St. Paul and the Vipers, by Lionella Spada
Courtesy of the Santa Barbara Museum of Art, Women's Board Purchase

Felix and Drusilla sat in their regal garments to listen to Paul. Drusilla may have then recalled her father's attitude toward James, whose death he ordered. They listened to Paul.

> And as he [Paul] argued about justice and self-control and future judgment, Felix was alarmed and said, "Go away for the present; when I have an opportunity I will summon you." At the same time he hoped that money would be given him by Paul. So he sent for him often and conversed with him. (Acts 24:25-26)

Imagine how the royal couple squirmed as Paul talked of justice and self-control. They were living in adultery. They were bribers and schemers in obtaining gifts. They were descended from immoral, cruel ancestors. They were pompous outwardly and empty inwardly, like scarecrows in beautiful garments. Drusilla did not really want to know that the Christ had come. What would she have done with him? Felix ended the hearing abruptly.

Paul spent the next two years in prison in Caesarea. Off and on during this time, riots between Jews and Greeks raged in the city. The Jews were victorious. But Felix sent his troops to help the Greeks. They killed thousands of Jews. Felix's troops sacked the homes of rich Jews.

The Jews told Rome of Felix's unfairness to them. As a result, the emperor ordered Felix out of Caesarea. Paul stayed in prison. There Porcius Festus, Felix's successor, found him in A.D. 59 or 60.

FESTUS, AGRIPPA II, BERNICE . . . AND PAUL
Acts 25:1-27

Felix was banished from Judea, and Porcius Festus replaced him. After three days in his royal city, Caesarea, Festus went up to Jerusalem. The Jews made the same three charges against Paul to Festus as they had made to Felix: sedition, heresy, sacrilege. Festus ordered a trial to be held within two weeks in Caesarea. When Festus came back to Caesarea, he asked Paul if he wanted to return to Jerusalem to be tried. But Paul replied:

> "I am standing before Caesar's tribunal, where I ought to be tried. . . . I appeal to Caesar." Then Festus, when he had conferred with his council, answered, "You have appealed to Caesar; to Caesar you shall go." (Acts 25:10-12)

We wonder if Paul might not have wanted this situation in some ways. At least he now had a chance to go to Rome, the capital city of the empire. He must have yearned to witness of his Lord to Roman senators and even to the emperor Nero. Suppose he could convert some senators, or even Nero. What a change in the empire such conversions would make! Paul must have rejoiced over the thought of going to Rome to be tried by his emperor. Had he not been on trial many times before? Had he not used each trial as a time to witness that Jesus is the Messiah? Surely the night air must have vibrated with the sound of Paul singing psalms.

> Now when some days had passed, Agrippa the king and Bernice arrived at Caesarea to welcome Festus. And as they stayed there many days, Festus laid Paul's case before the king. . . .
>
> So on the morrow Agrippa and Bernice came with great pomp, and they entered the audience hall with the military tribunes and the prominent men of the city. Then by command of Festus Paul was brought in. (Acts 25:13-14, 23)

Who were the people in this new scene? King Agrippa II was the brother of his mistress, Bernice. He was also the brother of Drusilla, the wife of Felix. (Acts 24) Bernice had married her uncle, Herod, king of Chalcis. Later she left him and returned to her brother, Herod Agrippa II. With him she lived incestuously. Later she also became the mistress of Titus, the man who captured Judea about A.D. 68-70. Paul was brought before this couple, Agrippa II and Bernice, his sister-mistress.

What a contrast in men! Agrippa grew up in Rome. He was a Hellenized Jew. He had lived in the luxury and elegance of Roman culture, with its music, oratory, women, sports, and arms. He was a son of the famous Herod family. He was devoted to worldly values—money, possessions, extortion, sex, and the spoils of conquest.

Paul, on the other hand, grew up a strict Jew in Tarsus and Jerusalem. His mission work had taken him across the empire. He knew risk, hazard, torture, pain, anger, and peril. For Paul the world was alive with God. Paul's values opposed those of the king. He looked forward to the unity of mankind in Christ. Within that unity God will include Jew and Gentile, slave and free, man and woman. All are to become one in Christ. These aims are spiritual values. And they were unlike the worldly values of Agrippa II. Paul looked for the coming of the kingdom of God. Agrippa saw only the military might of chariots and weapons. Paul saw a new world being born in Jesus Christ. A new mankind was coming to birth. New persons in Christ were making the world new. Some were turning the world upside down. This new world was coming because God's promises to Abraham, Isaac, Jacob, Joseph, Joshua, David, and the prophets were carried out by the risen Christ. So when Agrippa allowed Paul to speak, Paul spoke of his own faith. (Acts 26:1) He *witnessed* to these three royal leaders as they sat on their thrones.

PAUL'S WITNESS TO HIS KING
Acts 26:1-32

| And now I stand here on trial for hope in the promise made by
God to our fathers, to which our twelve tribes hope to attain, as
they earnestly worship night and day. (Acts 26:6-7)

Agrippa and Bernice were Jews, though immoral ones. They understood Paul's words about "our fathers." They knew the covenant. They knew Deuteronomy 6:5-9, their creed. They had said it by heart hundreds of times. They had prayed in the temple for the coming of the Messiah. And Paul declared that their prayers were answered. The Messiah had come.

Paul's witness to these rulers included telling about his past as a persecutor. He shared his vision of Christ on the Damascus road. He told them how the risen Christ appeared to him. Then he told with beauty what Christ had come to do for men.

| ". . . to open their eyes, that they may turn from darkness to
light and from the power of Satan to God, that they may receive
forgiveness of sins and a place among those who are sanctified
by faith in me [Christ]." (Acts 26:18)

In this speech we see four things that Christ does for men. (1) He opens their eyes. When Christ enters a person, that person sees life as he has never seen it before. After the burning bush, Moses could never look at a bush again without thinking of God's presence. Ezekiel could never see a sandstorm without thinking of God. Some biologists look at the make-up of living tissues and declare that the whole earth is full of the glory of God. (2) Christ turns men from darkness to light. Some walk with their backs to the light. So they walk in their own shadows. God is light, and Christ helps a person to live fully in God's light. (3) Christ turns a person from the power of Satan to the power of God. A stingy Zacchaeus repays fourfold. (Luke 19:2) A sex-possessed Magdalene finds the beauty of holiness. Unstable Legion finds peace and poise. A Jewish fanatic becomes the loyal apostle of Christ to the Gentiles. (4) Christ offers forgiveness of sins and a new life. Forgiveness means that the old life is left behind, dead and forgotten. A new future lies ahead. The risen Christ, Paul proclaimed, calls men into a new day.

Festus was getting embarrassed. "Festus said with a loud voice, 'Paul, you are mad; your great learning is turning you mad.'" (Acts 26:24) What a clever step when Paul turned to the Jew, King Agrippa II, and asked him to tell Festus that he was not mad.

| "I am not mad, most excellent Festus, but I am speaking the sober
truth. For the king knows about these things, and to him I speak
freely; for I am persuaded that none of these things has escaped

his notice, for this was not done in a corner. King Agrippa, do you believe the prophets? I know that you believe." (Acts 26:25-27)

Agrippa changed the subject quickly. He may have resented having Paul appeal to him against Festus. Paul would have rejoiced to have King Agrippa become a Christian and win Festus to the faith.

Then Paul said, "I would to God that not only you but also all who hear me this day might become such as I am." (Acts 26:29) He meant, "I wish you knew Christ as I do." He might have said: "If only you could meet the risen Lord. If only you knew what I have experienced!"

No doubt Agrippa meant it when he later said, "This man is doing nothing to deserve death or imprisonment." (Acts 26:31) But Paul's appeal to Caesar could not be withdrawn legally. Agrippa could not release him.

PAUL MINISTERS IN ROME
Acts 27:1 through 28:31

Finally Paul left Caesarea for Italy. He sailed as a prisoner under the authority of "a centurion named Julius." He was accompanied by two Christian companions. He eventually witnessed to the emperor.

At Myra, Paul changed vessels and boarded a corn ship from Alexandria. It was a ship of the Roman Empire's merchant marine. It carried food supplies from the rich soil of the Nile to Rome. As the weeks went by, the ship was caught in a severe storm. The passengers and crew were seasick for weeks. (See Acts 27:21-33.) At the depths of despair, Paul had another vision of the risen Christ. He tried to encourage other persons on the ship.

"I now bid you take heart; for there will be no loss of life among you, but only of the ship. For this very night there stood by me an angel of the God to whom I belong and whom I worship, and he said, 'Do not be afraid, Paul; you must stand before Caesar; and lo, God has granted you all those who sail with you.' So take heart, men, for I have faith in God that it will be exactly as I have been told." (Acts 27:22-25)

Over the noise of the waves crashing and the ship rocking, with everyone weary and seasick, Paul brought the first good news for weeks. He knew that the God of the fathers had been with him again. Courage. Emmanuel! He knew God's purpose for him would prevail. He would see Caesar.

Paul's certainty was based on his confidence in *Scripture*. God "measured the waters in the hollow of his hand." (Isaiah 40:12) He assured the faithful that "underneath are the everlasting arms."

(Deuteronomy 33:27) *Traditions* of the fathers proclaimed God's guiding hand on pilgrims of faith such as Joseph, who knew that God acted through his life for the good of others. *Experience* of three shipwrecks and many other times of stress showed Paul that God was with him and planned other things for him. And Paul's *reason* agreed that the God who acted redemptively in the past could be expected to do so again. No, God did not save the company from shipwreck. But he did save every one of the 276 lives.

Finally, three months after the company had been shipwrecked on Malta, they arrived in Italy. Some brethren from Rome met Paul. They had come thirty miles to greet him. They had received his Letter to the Romans, and they yearned to see him and to talk with him. The Greek word for *came to meet us* (Acts 28:15) is the same word used of a deputation that goes out to meet a conquering hero or king. Luke wants us to realize that Paul's friends from Rome came with a greeting of honor. Hail the conquering hero. Truly he was one of the great men of the earth.

Paul lived in Rome for two years at his own expense. Apparently he was under guard and not allowed to leave Rome during this time. But he was not in a prison. His companions were Luke, Aristarchus, Timothy, Tychicus, Epaphroditus, and Mark. Mark finally came back to Paul after being with Barnabas those many years. Paul was busy during these two years. He wrote the letters we call Philippians, Ephesians, Colossians, and Philemon. He preached to many citizens of Rome and to the soldiers who guarded him. They were the picked troops of the emperor, the Praetorian Guard. He spent long days and nights with them. We can well imagine what they discussed. And we can imagine some baptisms too.

Luke's record closes before we see Paul standing before Caesar. His witness must have been similar to what he said before King Agrippa II. Dependable legends say that Paul was found guilty and beheaded.

Let us conclude our study with the words of a great Christian, Clement of Rome, who wrote two decades after Paul died. "Paul won the noble glory of his faith. He taught righteousness to all the world, and when he had reached the limit of the west he gave his testimony before rulers, and thus passed from the world and was taken up into the Holy Place, the greatest example of endurance."

But exceeding the greatness of Paul was the greatness of his Lord, Jesus Christ. Paul never would have boasted of his own achievements. His boast was about Christ. "For me to live is Christ. . . ," he wrote. (Philippians 1:21) This was his real achievement. Men found Christ through Paul.

Questions for Discussion
Chapter 1

1. Why is it important for us to know who wrote the various books of the Bible? Apply your answer to Acts.

2. What did Jesus teach about the Kingdom? (Read Matthew 13:24-33, 44-52.) How does the Kingdom come? When you pray, "Thy kingdom come," what are you praying for? What changes do you expect as a result of that prayer?

3. How did the disciples view the universe? What symbolism do we find in the story of the Ascension? What is the significance of the Ascension for us?

4. What promise did Jesus make at the time of his Ascension? What continuing value does that promise have for your faith today?

5. At the time of the Ascension, what promise did the "two men . . . in white robes" make to the disciples? To what degree do you personally cherish this promise today? How would you compare Acts 1:10-11, Matthew 24:29-31, and John 14:3? What other passages in the New Testament speak of Christ returning to the earth?

6. What experiences qualified Matthias to become an apostle? What do you think of the method used by the disciples to choose Matthias? What, according to Acts 1:21-22, is the first and fundamental task of an apostle? In what sense is this still the chief task of the whole church?

Chapter 2

1. What promises did God fulfill when he gave his Holy Spirit to the church? What can you identify within the life of your church that is a sign of the Holy Spirit's presence?

2. What did the "tongues" of Pentecost represent? What gifts do you expect to find in a Spirit-filled church? (See 1 Corinthians 12 through 14 and Galatians 5:13-25.)

3. How does Paul distinguish between tongues and prophecy? Where do you look in your church to find and hear prophecy?

4. How would you repeat Peter's sermon in your own words? When we tell others of Jesus, what ideas about him must we include?

5. Why is Pentecost sometimes called the birthday of the church?

6. How does the celebration of Pentecost in your church pick up the meaning of Pentecost as you discover it in Acts 2? Why is red an appropriate color for the liturgical celebration of Pentecost?

7. What were the signs of the Spirit's presence in Jerusalem during and immediately after Pentecost? What did the "mighty wind" symbolize? What did the "tongues as of fire" represent?

8. What did the persons who composed the early church have in common? What qualified the first Christians for membership in the young church?

Chapter 3

1. How would you describe life in the early church? Viewing the early church as a model, ask yourself the following question: What chiefly is the proper business of the church?

2. How could the ministries of your congregation better reflect the compassion and power of the risen Christ?

3. Which one of the main ideas in Peter's sermon means the most to you? How useful to you is the word *covenant* in describing your own relationship to God?

4. What about Christianity did the Sadducees reject? What parallels to the conflict between Peter and the Sadducees do you see in modern life? How did the apostles pray in Acts 4:23-32? How does this prayer instruct our praying?

5. What can you say in favor of the actions taken by the Sadducees and their council (the Sanhedrin)? How can you reconcile Acts 5:29 to Mark 12:17? Why was Peter willing to obey God in spite of danger from the Sanhedrin? Why did conflict break out between the Hellenists and the Hebrews?

6. What was the purpose of communal sharing in the early church? What principle guided the distribution of property within the young church?

7. What do each of the following passages teach about the Holy Spirit: Matthew 28:19; 2 Corinthians 13:14; Hebrews 9:14; Romans 15:19; Luke 1:35; and 2 Peter 1:21?

8. What role did Gamaliel play in the persecution of the early church?

9. Who were the Hellenists? Who were the Hebrews? (Acts 6:1) What caused the tension between them in the Jerusalem church? What tensions in the modern church seem analogous to you?

Chapter 4

1. Who were Jews, Hebrews, and Hellenists? Are you, through your church, helping people with whom you would not ordinarily associate except for your love of Christ?

2. What charges were brought against Stephen? How many similarities can you find between the martyrdoms of Jesus and Stephen?

3. According to Stephen, how did Israel disobey God? As you read Stephen's speech, do you feel that the charges against him were valid? Does your congregation, like ancient Israel, resist the Holy Spirit? How do we oppose God's Spirit?

4. What about the life and death of Stephen do you find inspirational? What understanding of Christian witnessing do you gain from the speech and death of Stephen?

5. How did the persecution of the church contribute to the growth and spread of the church?

6. What portions of Stephen's defense remind you of the sayings of Jesus? What words of Jesus come to your mind as you read Stephen's speech? How do you compare Stephen's attitude toward the temple to John 4:20-24? What did Jesus say and do with respect to the temple? What meaning do "holy places" and houses for worship hold in modern Christianity?

7. How would you summarize Stephen's charges against the Jews before whom he was tried? What parallel charges might a modern prophet lodge against your congregation, if given a chance?

8. What do you suppose was the motive behind Saul's persecuting zeal?

Chapter 5

1. What signs do you see that Christ is present in your church today? What are the signs that Christ is present in American society today? If your chuch were more open to the Spirit, what new signs of his presence would you expect? (Refer to Colossians 3:1-17, especially verses 12-17.)

2. Simon thought he could buy spiritual power. What are some of the false ways to seek spiritual power today? What would the term *spiritual power* have meant to Simon the magician? What does the term *spiritual power* mean to you? What can you do to let the Spirit become more powerful in your own life?

3. What drove Philip to approach the eunuch? What prepared the eunuch to listen to Philip? Where did Philip get the insights he needed to instruct the eunuch? What made Philip's witness effective? How do you seek the drive and the insights to become a better witness?

4. How do you recognize Christ when he speaks to you? What form does his presence take in your life? How do his words come to you? How did he show you the work he has for you to do?

5. What did Paul believe about his own conversion? If Paul were born today as an apostle, what new mission might he undertake?

6. What definition of the word *miracle* best fits the use of that word in Acts 8:13? In our scientific age, how strongly should the church emphasize miracles in the promotion of the faith?

7. What passages from Acts would you include on a list designed to show the importance of the Holy Spirit in the church?

8. How was the prophecy in Acts 9:16 fulfilled in Paul's later life?

Chapter 6

1. What place did healing have in the ministry of the early church? How is faith healing a true ministry today? What forms does the healing ministry of the church take today? How does your church share in a healing ministry? How is the promise in John 14:12 being fulfilled in our day?

2. What kind of man was Cornelius? If Cornelius was already a man of integrity, prayer, charity, and high morality, what more could he expect to receive from Peter? Or from Christ? What does Christ give us that Cornelius did not have already?

3. Was God saying to Peter, "You may now ignore Leviticus 11:1-47"? What did the vision of Peter have to do with Cornelius? What moral rules guide the Christian in his choice of friends and associates? When is it moral to remain aloof from other people?

4. How might you paraphrase Peter's sermon to Cornelius? How can we know when the Word of God has been truly spoken? What should be the content of Christian preaching? What ideas, if any, should appear in every Christian sermon? How do you decide if a sermon is biblical? How could you help your minister become a stronger preacher?

5. What steps can you take to help the church include everyone?

6. How does the conversion of Cornelius mark a new phase in the spread of the gospel? How do you account for the fact that surprising and sudden conversions are rare in mainline Protestant churches today?

7. What new insights did Peter gain as a result of the entire Cornelius episode? Which of these insights need to be renewed or revived in your congregation? Why?

Chapter 7

1. How did persecution in Jerusalem cause the gospel to spread to Antioch? What social forces in your town tend to stifle the spread of the gospel?

2. In Antioch the church was working in new places and in new ways. Are there "new places" and "new ways" for the church to work today? What "new places" has your church entered? What "new ways" has your church tried? What have been your own feelings about new forms of service, worship, and witness?

3. Three words that describe the work of a clergyman are *prophet, priest,* and *pastor.* What does each of these words say to you about the proper work of the ministry?

4. How does evil grow when it is encouraged? What passages in the New Testament help you know how a Christian should bear persecution? What form has persecution taken in your life?

5. Why is prayer an important part of the Christian life? How is prayer a valid approach to change in today's world?

6. How does God deal with his enemies?

7. Why was Barnabas sent from Jerusalem to Antioch? What does his mission indicate about the authority of the church in Jerusalem? What are the values in having a clear, centralized authority in the church (or a denomination)? Where today is the authority formerly exercised by the twelve apostles? How was their authority passed on to the church of later ages?

8. When did it first become apparent that Christianity was a new religion rather than merely a minor Jewish sect? What form of reconciliation should Christians seek with Jews today?

Chapter 8

1. Why do we go to those we do not know to share our faith? Is the Christian faith better than all other religious systems? If so, why? If not, why not? The prophets in Antioch fasted and then heard the Spirit. How do we get ready to hear and accept divine guidance?

2. What forms of magic are real today? How is superstition like magic? What form does magic take in our world? How is astrology like magic? How is spiritualism like magic? How is gambling like magic? When does prayer become a form of magic?

3. What did Paul tell the Jews of Antioch about Jesus? How does Paul claim that Jesus is the goal of Jewish history? This sermon is Paul's way of telling who Jesus is and what he means. How would you put into words the meaning of Jesus for you?

4. What meaning do you see in the ceremony described in Acts 13:3 ("Then after fasting and praying they laid their hands on them and sent them off")? What ceremonies are used in your church in order to set persons apart for special tasks? How might special services be used in your church to commission or dedicate laymen for special tasks?

5. In what ways was Syrian Antioch uniquely suited to become a base for the great missionary journeys of Paul?

6. Why did Paul, in his missionary preaching, always preach first in a Jewish synagogue before addressing the Gentile population? On what frontiers should the missionary efforts of the church today be concentrated?

7. What ideas appear in both Peter's sermon at Pentecost (Acts 2:14-39) and Paul's sermon in Antioch (Acts 13:16-41)? What significant facets of the Christian faith seem to be omitted from these two sermons?

Chapter 9

1. What do you make of the idea that each of us must enter the Kingdom through suffering? How does your church bolster the faith of new converts?

2. Why did the former Pharisees urge Jewish law upon all Christians? How do we know they were wrong when they did this? Why did Paul and Barnabas turn to the church in Jerusalem for a decision? What do you think Paul would have done if the decision in Jerusalem had gone against him?

3. What did the Jerusalem Council decide? How does this decision apply to Christians today? How does your church invite the guidance of the Spirit as decisions are made by boards and committees?

4. What feelings do you have when you read about sharp divisions and arguments among saintly men like Paul and Barnabas? How does your Bible class try to reconcile differences within the group?

5. What to this point in Acts are the most striking traits in Paul's character and personality? What qualities, if any, appear in his personality that should appear in every Christian personality? Which of these following traits would you ascribe to Paul: fortitude, tenderness, perseverance, sympathy, wisdom, patience, pride, willfulness, diplomacy, fairness? Account for your answer by referring to his words or actions.

6. At the Jerusalem Council, how was Gentile Christianity defended? What were those Christians defending who insisted that Gentile converts to Christ must keep the Jewish laws? What does it mean to be *saved* by *grace?*

7. Tell why you agree (or disagree) with this statement: Divisions in the church *always* indicate a deficiency of faith *and* love.

Chapter 10

1. Which passages in Acts tell us that the Holy Spirit directed Paul's work? How does God speak to people today? What part do dreams and visions play in making a better life? How does God usually guide you?

2. How did Paul affect his jailer? What was the source of Paul's courage? When has your loyalty to Christ demanded courage? What conflicts have you faced because of your faith? Include both inner and outer conflicts in your answer.

3. How did the people in Thessalonica react to Paul's message? Notice in Acts 17:2-3 that Paul based his message upon Scripture and little else. How might ministers today teach God's Word more fully? How might your church use the Bible more often in preaching, teaching, worship, and evangelism?

4. What are the main ideas in Paul's sermon at Athens? Intellectual pride stopped the Greek philosophers from accepting Paul's message. What is intellectual pride? What causes it? Why is intellectual pride a barrier to the gospel? Can you tell of a time when intellectual pride held you back from repentance or faith?

5. What charges against Paul led to the beating he received in Philippi? What analogous charges have been lodged against Christian preachers in our day? How did patriotism enter into the charges against Paul? What is the relationship between Christian ethics and our own national customs?

6. In your judgment is the preaching of the Christian faith ever politically dangerous? If so, why?

7. How would you describe the strategy or psychology of Paul's speech in Athens? What use should preaching today make of insights derived from the psychology of salesmanship?

Chapter 11

1. What have you learned about Paul's health and his trade? Suppose all ministers earned their own way apart from the church, as Paul did. How might this be good? How might this be bad?

2. What can Christians learn from Jews today? What can Jews learn from Christians today? Are Jews still, in any sense, God's special people? Should the church today pray and work for the conversion of the Jews? If your class wishes to follow these questions further, study Romans 9 through 11. Recall a time when the risen Christ (or the Holy Spirit) spoke to you. In what form did he appear? Through what medium did his message come? By what signs do you know that God is close to you? to your church?

3. How might God use our nation to help spread the gospel? What does our nation do that might slow down the spread of the gospel?

4. Who was Apollos, and what did he do?

5. How many examples of "magic" can you discover in your world today? Are some religious practices really only "magic" in disguise? As you answer, follow the definition of "magic" as man's effort to control supernatural powers for selfish ends.

6. In general, what attitude did Roman officials take toward the promotion and promulgation of Christianity, as far as Acts tells? In your judgment should our government (at various levels) remain neutral in all matters of religion? Or should our government promote Christian values without favoring any one church? How should our government treat religions that promote values that are contrary to Christian values?

7. Do you see in Acts 19:12 a basis for the Roman Catholic practice of ascribing special powers to the relics of saints? What continuing meaning does such a verse have for a Protestant?

Chapter 12

1. You have now read about Ephesus. Earlier you read about Corinth, Antioch, and Athens. How would you compare these four cities to one another? Think now about your own town, country, or city. What conditions in your town make a Christian witness difficult? What conditions encourage a Christian witness?

2. What caused the riot in Ephesus? Demetrius was a silversmith. His business was threatened by the Christian Way. What professions or businesses in our society are threatened by the Christian Way?

3. Paul believed that men are saved by grace through faith. Which events from Paul's life show you most clearly the size of his faith?

4. Some Jews attacked Paul to defend their temple. They used violence to guard their religion. When have Christians defended their religion violently? Are there any circumstances that make violence necessary in the defense of faith? Should military power be used by Christian nations to defend the Christian religion?

5. The risen Lord gave Paul guidance. The Holy Spirit often guided the early church at crucial moments. How does guidance come to the church today? How does the risen Lord guide you today?

6. What guidelines and motives drawn from the Christian faith ought a businessman take into his profession? What sacrifices might a businessman make in order to keep from compromising his Christian principles?

7. Why did Paul continue to observe the main Jewish feasts (as Acts 20:16 implies)? Under what circumstances might Jews and Christians benefit from worshiping together?

8. Acts 20:17-35 is Paul's own summary of his obedience to the gospel. How might a similar summary based on your life read? Write one.

Chapter 13

1. What did Paul say to Felix that is for you most inspiring? Recall a time when you were the object of false charges. How did your faith help you respond to your accusers with love and courage?

2. How should a Christian behave when he is persecuted? (Base your answer on the example of Paul.) After reading Acts 25, what feelings do you have about the character of Festus?

3. Did you ever turn a moment of trial (or testing) into a moment of witnessing? Tell about it.

4. As you recall the whole of Acts, how would you describe the personality of Paul? What do you admire most about Paul?

5. Why did Paul appeal his case to Caesar? What rebuttal might you offer to this claim: It is strategically more important to preach the gospel to powerful leaders than to little people who have no influence or following?

6. How often in the Book of Acts do we notice the advantages Paul gained from his Roman citizenship? What other cases can you recall when God seemed to use a person's social background to further the gospel? Are there any human gifts, talents, or accomplishments that God cannot use to promote his own cause? Explain your answer.

7. According to Acts 26, what did Paul learn from his encounter with Christ on the road to Damascus? Does any man have the right to make the unqualified claim that Paul makes in Acts 26:19? Why might we doubt that any man is ever totally obedient to his "heavenly vision"? How basic to your faith is the word *obedience?* What examples can you give of the meaning *obedience* has in your life?